"*An absolute must read* †

Lara Morgan, CEO Company Shortcuts

Heels of *Steel*

Surviving & Thriving in the Corporate World

VANESSA VALLELY

Heels of Steel

First published in 2013 by Panoma Press

48 St Vincent Drive, St Albans, Herts, AL1 5SJ, UK

info@panomapress.com
www.panomapress.com

Cover Design by Martyn Paris. Book layout by Neil Coe.

Printed on acid-free paper from managed forests. This book is printed on demand to fulfill orders, so no copies will be remaindered or pulped.

ISBN 978-1-909623-11-8

For the Pipeline of future talent

For those already on the journey

For those who told me I couldn't

For my girls, Mia and Ella, may you
never face such challenges

For Mum and Dad, what didn't break us
made us stronger

For Stewart, as without you, I am nothing

PRAISE FOR THIS BOOK

As with everything about Vanessa, she has generously opened up her heart and soul to share her fascinating life story and the lessons she has learnt along the way. Her story shows that with self awareness and emotional intelligence, you can triumph through any adversity to fulfil your ambitions. Her tips for success are pragmatic and easy to follow, as she says 'don't just survive it, thrive in it!'

**Fleur Bothwick, OBE | Ernst & Young,
Director of Diversity & Inclusive Leadership - EMEIA**

There is so much that can be learnt from Vanessa's journey – she is an inspirational role model and her story shows that we can achieve anything if we are bold enough to dream it and brave enough to work hard earning it.

Ruby McGregor-Smith, CBE, CEO, MITIE Group PLC

Vanessa's personal story reads like a roller coaster ride with dynamic cast of characters, I couldn't turn the pages fast enough to find out what happened next! Her advice to others clearly comes from the heart as well as from considerable experience. I'm sure she will inspire the next generations coming through to think about their career and life plans in different ways.

Birgit Neu, MD, Neuchange

An inspirational human story, I couldn't put it down, Vanessa helps you gather strength for your own experiences through her own, one to own

Andy Woodfield, Partner, PWC

Vanessa sets out her journey in a very clear and entertaining way. As she says, we learn as much from her mistakes as we do from her many successes.

Vanessa's advice, to recognise when your body is telling you to have a break from hard work, is spot on, and so is her suggestion that we regularly take stock of where we are and where we want to go.

Carole Stone, Author,
Networking – the art of making friends

This is the fascinating story of a powerhouse entrepreneurial women in the corporate world. Vanessa Vallely is one of the most smartest networkers I know because she comes from the heart as well as the head. Don't miss the chance to read her book and how she lives and works.

Lynne Franks, Founder of SEED Women's Network and B.Hive Women's Business Clubs

In recounting her life story; 'the good, the bad and the ugly' Vanessa demonstrates the power of vulnerability and openness. She establishes her credibility as an engaging and generous leader.

It is through her resilience, readiness to learn from her mistakes, commitment to her values and sharing her wisdom that she provides invaluable guidance, strategies and resources for anyone who wants to determine, set and achieve their goals in a corporate environment.

Sylvana Caloni, Founder, SC Executive Coaching and President, Women In Banking & Finance

Congratulations - at last we have our own homegrown Oprah Winfrey in Vanessa! This book is a great career navigator for every youngster who has been told they can't achieve!

Heather Melville, Regional Sales Director, Global Chair and founder of the 10,000 +p RBS Women's Network, Focused Women

Heels of Steel is two books in one.... and they are both winners. There are so many lessons to be learnt from Vanessa's inspirational journey, yet she doesn't rest there. After sharing her route to success Vanessa goes on to outline exactly what she has learnt on the way and gives the reader practical steps to take to avoid mistakes and learn from her experience.

A must read for anyone wanting to climb the corporate ladder....or simply to support those who do.

Andy Lopata, Author of 'Recommended', '...and Death Came Third!' and 'Building a Business on Bacon and Eggs'

Vanessa has never lost the sense of where she came from. Guts got her there. Determination and hard work kept her there. But her many admirers and mentees in the City know she cares and shares. Not so much heels of steel but heart of gold.

Lady Val Corbett

Vanessa is a testament TO THE FACT THAT inner strength overcomes the inner city, an inspiration for every young girl whose dreams go beyond a Disney fairy tale.

Sue O'Brien - CEO UK, Norman Broadbent

With thanks to:

Chantelle Akerman, Foluke Akinsola MBE, Analisa Balares, Maggie Berry, Marlise Bilham, Fleur Bothwick, Eileen Brown, Sonia Brown MBE, Racheal Butcher, Sylvana Caloni, Liz Campbell, Tracey Carr, John Cassidy, Louise Chester Cox, Yasmine Chinwala, John Christner, Angela Clements, Chantal Constable, Lady Val Corbett, Roy Dainty, Ms Dene, Suzanne Doyle Morris, Leonnie Fisher, Paul Forster, Hannah Foxley, Lynne Franks, Farida Gibbs, Letty Gibbs, Diane Greenidge, John Hodgson, Nicola Horlick, Cherie Huffman, Christina Ioannidis, Nayan Kisnadwala, Rajesh Lad, Ronke Lawal, Christine Lawrence, Nick & Hannah Lindsay, Katherine Loe, Arnold Longboy, Andy Lopata, Nick Lloyd, Justine Lutterodt, Amanda Mackenzie, Ruby McGregor-Smith, David McQueen, Duncan McRae, Ali Meehan, Heather Melville, Lara Morgan, Sandra Murphy, Birgit Neu, Pippa Nutley, Victor Nutley, Sue O'Brien, Debbie O'Hara, Lynne Parker, Claudia Parrinello, Amanda Phillips, Mr Purcell, Sarah Quinn, Melanie Reynolds, Simone Roche, Grace Ross, Lisanne Schloss, Dania Seglie, Maggie Semple MBE, Fiona Severs, Owen Sharp, Sam Shaw, Sandie Small, Tracey Stevens, Carole Stone, Susan Syme, Amie Tierney, TNON Members, Ella Vallely, Mia Vallely, Stewart Vallely, Andy Woodfield, Heather White, Nooshin White, Kay White, WeAreTheCity Members.

For making this book a reality:

Birgit Neu. The editorial and design team at Panoma. Mindy Gibbins-Klein from The Book Midwife for her support and belief in my book. Emma Herbert for her passion and patience. Helen Lewis at Literally PR for all her hard work. My mum for our endless Sundays spent proofreading and above all for allowing me to share our story. To Stewart and my girls for giving me the time to make my dream of writing this book a reality.

CONTENTS

Foreword - Nicola Horlick

Barely a day goes by without the issue of women in the workplace being discussed in newspapers and on radio and television. Over the thirty years that I have been working, expectations have changed dramatically. It is now the norm for young women to achieve 9-11 GCSEs, 3-4 'A' levels and then go to university. Women are dominant on university courses such as law and medicine where the entry requirements are most stringent.

I went to Oxford in 1979 and it was a momentous year for the university. It was the year that the majority of the male colleges opened their doors to women. In the case of my own college, Balliol, is currently celebrating its 750th anniversary and yet there have only have been female members for 34 out of those 750 years. There is no question that women have made a great deal of progress in recent years and yet they are still underrepresented at consultant level in medicine with some areas such as surgery remaining the province of men, and there are very few female partners in the major City law firms. This pattern is reflected in business, where there remains low representation for women at board level.

Given the success of girls at school and university, it is hard to comprehend why their success has been poor in the work place. There are really only two possible reasons for this. The first could be that women do not want to put themselves in a position of responsibility, preferring to remain in the so-called marzipan layer. It may well be that they are happy to head up a team and nurture those within it, but they do not want the stress and pressure that comes with being in overall charge of a company or organisation.

The second possible reason is that there are so few women in top positions in the UK could be that men do not want them there. Is there a glass ceiling or not? My own experience has been that there isn't. I started my career in the City in 1983 after having working for a family business for a year. Within six years, I had been made a director. Two years later, I was headhunted by another major bank and was given a top role and a year after that was Chief Executive of the UK investment business and on the main board of the asset management division. This was at a time when the City was totally male dominated and there were very few senior women and I was already the mother of three children.

Looking back, I was extremely fortunate to start my career at a bank, S. G. Warburg, which was totally meritocratic. This ethos had led to extraordinary success as the bank was only founded post-war and yet was dominant in most areas by the time I came to the City. I was lucky enough to be invited to the final round of interviews at several merchant banks and it was clear to me, just from going through that process, that there was something very different about Warburgs. At the other banks, I was the only woman present and the only one who had not been to Eton or Winchester. Everyone present was British and everyone had been to either Oxford or Cambridge. By contrast, at Warburgs, there were equal numbers of women and men being interviewed, they came from all over the world and had diverse educational experiences. I could instantly see why Warburgs had been so successful and immediately accepted when I was offered a place on the graduate training scheme.

Part of my early career success was due to making the right choice in terms of my employer, but equally, the realisation that you need a sponsor who is powerful in the organisation helped me immensely. Like all things in life, luck played a major part.

I am certain that women can progress quickly to senior positions if they manage their careers in the right way. The problem is that few do manage their careers properly and tend to take the view that, if they work really hard and keep their heads down, someone will eventually notice. Sadly, this is not always the case. I remain convinced that it is essential to have a sponsor in a large organisation.

I enormously admire Vanessa's achievements and when she asked me to write something for her book, I was very flattered. She left school at 15 and did not have the benefit of the education that I received. The City is a forbidding place, but she had the guts and determination to go in there and succeed against all the odds. She has gone on to establish a networking organisation that has become a vital part of life in the City for its female workers. Women can greatly benefit from encouragement and support from their peers and Vanessa has created a way for them to gain this.

This book chronicles the ups and downs of Vanessa's career and anyone reading it, irrespective of whether they work in financial services, will gain something.

Introduction

As a six-year-old child I spent a lot of time looking out from the 18th floor window of our tower block in Hoxton in London's East End towards the bright lights of the City's financial district. "One day I am going to work in one of those tall buildings," I said to my mum. "I will have a big office like the ones we clean, and things will be different for us."

As I got older, I realised that my dreams would only ever come to fruition if I got off my backside and worked hard. Armed with drive, passion and a cheap suit I entered the City at age 15 determined to make a name for myself in the corporate world. I knew it would be tough for me because I didn't leave school with a great academic record, nor was I the norm in terms of my background. What I did have was faith in myself, and a belief that if I truly put enough effort in, I would succeed and life would indeed be different for my mum and me.

Achieving career success took me considerably longer than I expected. I attribute this to two factors in my case. The first factor was undoubtedly the impact of pausing to have two beautiful children mid-career. The second factor, which I think played a bigger role, was the fact that I started my career without having any insights about what it takes to succeed in the corporate world.

The very purpose of writing this book is to ensure that those of you who are part of the future talent pool can benefit from what I learned through my experiences, and that you can get a better understanding of the various ways that you can vault potential career hurdles and expedite your own success.

I know all about the challenges and pitfalls working women face first hand, I expect some of these are the same for men too. There is the constant search for recognition, the need for balance, and the quest to get to the point where you feel you actually have a clear direction for your career.

Before I go on to tell you the story of my own turbulent career and give you my advice, it's important for you to understand that I'm the first person to recognise that I haven't always made the right decisions or done things the appropriate way. There are stories within this book which I hope will inspire you to reflect on what didn't go right as opposed to what did. How would you have handled these situations? The learning is often not in what you read, but how what you read provokes thoughts and ideas in your own mind.

If I could go back and revisit any aspect of my own life or work experience I wouldn't change a thing. Not only am I extremely proud of my roots in London's East End, I am also exceptionally proud of what I've accomplished and learned by being in the corporate world over the past 25 years.

The first half of this book is the story of my life, with lumps, bumps, family and work all included. It is this 25-year experience that I leverage in the second half of the book to give you some suggestions as to how you can adopt some of what I have learned professionally to progress your own career at greater speed.

In spite of what others might have you believe, there are many individuals like me and organisations who want to help you achieve your potential; however, the time investment, passion and drive to make your success happen must come from you. Seek out our experience – use individuals like me and these amazing organisations as advisors and mentors. Hold us to account in terms of sharing our skills, experiences and above all our connections to help you find your way.

I have written this book not just to impart advice or tell my own corporate story, but because I want to encourage all my readers to think about the next generation, the pipeline! Regardless of how old you are, what experience you believe you have or where you are in your career, I want to encourage you to seek opportunities to support the next generation in some way – be it by mentoring, guidance, or purely by opening doors. These individuals need our support as they are ultimately the legacy we leave behind. They will also be the ones who go on potentially to take positions on our boards and contribute towards repairing our economy.

On a personal level, the challenge I set you outside of helping others is to start thinking about your own story. It could well be that you already know about all of the tips I impart later on in the book however, my question to you is are you actively practising them? Are you making time to do all the things you know you should be doing in order to take your career or business to the next level? Are you dedicating at least 10% of your working week to learning new things or meeting new people? If not, then I hope this book encourages you to think about whether these are activities you wish to engage in, because if you are serious about your career or business, then they should be!

It just remains for me to wish you well and encourage you to keep pushing your own boundaries. Above all, never give up on your big dreams; with a little bit of hard work, passion and dedication, achieving them is often closer than you think!

Vanessa

A HUMBLE START

From as early as I can remember, my mum and I drifted from one drama to another in a seemingly endless rotation of changing schools, changing jobs or brainstorming survival strategies for our family of two.

My mum met my dad at the tender age of 16. She was an intelligent young lady from a decent Jewish background. Despite losing her father when she was 11, she remained on the path to 'doing something' in life. She lived in London's East End with her mother, Nettie, who ran a successful business selling second-hand books in a market in Soho, and despite being from a one-parent family, by most measures my mum's life was OK.

My dad was from a family of 10 and he was East End through and through. Life for my dad was about surviving his latest scrape and, incongruously, raising money for charity through his role as a Pearly King. That role came to him through my paternal grandfather, George, who was also a Pearly King.

The Pearly Kings and Queens are known as the East End's alternative royal family. The Pearlies are individuals who wear suits adorned with buttons who raise money for charity across the various boroughs of London. This practice was started by an orphan boy by the name of Henry Croft in the early 1900s. Henry was a rat catcher who worked across the many markets that existed in London at the time. While he was working he would also raise pennies for the needy and his own orphanage. Henry was fascinated by the buttons the apple sellers (known as 'costers' from 'costermonger', which means seller of fruit and vegetables) sewed on to the lapels and trousers on their suits, so he decided to make a suit of his own that was completely covered in buttons so he would be recognisable as a charity worker within the markets. Henry became so popular that he was in demand across the many markets of London, a demand he was unable to service being just one man. He solved his problem by making a Pearly King or Queen for each of the 28 boroughs of London (including Westminster, City of London, Tower Hamlets and more). It then became the responsibility of that Pearly King or Queen to raise money for people within that borough. My dad, in spite of his other youthful interests, took his responsibilities as a Pearly King seriously. All of my family members on my dad's side wore buttons whether they liked it or not, it was our family's tradition.

When my mum and dad met I had no doubt they loved each other however, in hindsight, they were far too young to settle down. The idea for them to rush into marriage was more my paternal grandmother, Sadie's idea than it ever was theirs. That said, my mum was becoming increasingly persuaded by my Nan as this meant she could move away from her strict upbringing and start life on her own two feet. From my father's perspective, he would be the first to admit that he didn't want to get married, he was a young boy who wanted to do what young boys do – enjoy his early years and have fun with his mates. It was while having fun with his friends that he was involved in a terrible accident which left him with severe burns to his lower back, bottom and legs.

He was compensated for his fairly extensive burns, and with that money and Sadie's wish for her son to settle down, the idea for their wedding became a reality. My mum and dad were just 18 and 19 years old respectively at that point.

Nettie was horrified when she learned that my mum was planning to marry my dad. She never liked him and, in her eyes, he was never going to be good enough for her daughter.

Sadie, on the other hand, was just happy to be settling one of the last of her 10 children, and she hoped that he would become more responsible when he married my mother. They were married in 1970 at St. Martin-in-the-Fields, a huge church located in the centre of London, just off Trafalgar Square. The wedding was a grand affair, and guests and press came from far and wide to see all the Pearly Kings and Queens gather for this alternative royal wedding.

Nettie was still intent on stopping the wedding. On the eve of the big day she travelled to see my mum and offered her £500 in cash, a deposit on a house and a car in a bid to persuade her not to marry. This was quite an offer in 1970. Needless to say, my mum was intent on making her own way in life, and she went ahead with the wedding regardless. Two years later I was born, weighing in at a whopping 10lbs. and earning a name for myself as the biggest baby born in the hospital in five years. It was my very first award!

Given my parents' naivety and youth, it was only a matter of time before the responsibility of being married dawned on them and the novelty of being a couple with little income wore off. Nettie offered no support. In her view, my mum had made her bed and she now had to lie in it.

When I was just 10 weeks old my mum and dad separated, and by the time I was 10 months old they were divorced, leaving my mum to bring me up on her own, up to her eyes in their collective debt.

My first-ever childhood memory of living in the tower block was when I was five. It was a dark and dingy place where the lifts hardly ever worked and it smelt of urine. We would often have to walk up 18 flights of stairs several times a day. The flat was functional and served its purpose. We didn't have much in terms of trimmings, but we had a lot of love and each other and, to be honest, that was all that mattered. Today, people would pay thousands for the view I had from my bedroom window; in fact, our council flat would probably now be described as an apartment in one of London's trendiest and most up-and-coming areas. For me and mum, though, it felt more like a prison, one from which we were desperate to escape.

My mum always worked, so most of my time after school was spent with various carers and childminders. My mum struggled to find childcare for me in the early years and she went through various nightmares until she finally found someone she could trust. In those days anyone could call themselves a childminder, as the only primary qualification for doing so was having kids of your own.

One of the childminders I was with used to take the food my mum left her for me and use it to feed her own children. The last straw was when my mum noticed that not only was I always hungry when she picked me up, but various bruises had started to appear on my arms, legs and back. When my mum challenged the childminder, the childminder stated that I was a clumsy child and that I was always walking into things. My mum promptly removed me from her care as she knew that some of the bruising could not have been caused by the odd topple or fall. Luckily I don't remember any of it as I was too young, but I can only imagine the guilt she must have felt as a mother.

Like so many working mothers, she had no choice but to put me in the hands of other carers because she had to go to work. We had bills to pay and she refused to claim any form of benefit, so anything we wanted we would invariably have to work hard for.

My mum eventually found a childminder she trusted and enrolled me in the local school. It was a nice school but they taught an extremely odd curriculum where words were spelt phonetically. I was also forced to write with my right hand even though I'm naturally left-handed, so educationally things were not starting out too well.

I stayed in that school and in my new childminder's care for just over a year. During this time my mum had been campaigning at the housing department to get us moved out of the tower block. She had become so desperate that she threatened to throw herself off the top floor if they didn't move us. Given that she had a history of depression, they relocated us to a new council estate that had recently been built about a mile away. We were to be the proud tenants of a brand new two-bedroom maisonette. The best part was that there were only two flights of stairs! My mum said I was most overjoyed by the fact I wouldn't have to run down 36 flights of stairs to catch the ice cream van, only to come back with a melted ice cream!

Moving to the maisonette was a new beginning for us: a new school (yet again), a nice new home and a chance to make a fresh start. My dad had met wife number two by this point who, in all fairness, loved and treated me like one of her own. My dad's stability and his new wife's welcoming arms meant that I could see more of him, and I visited him every other weekend, and have continued to do so during the past 40 years.

School holidays were often spent in government-funded school camps or in the care of my grandparents. My grandparents on both sides of my family were owners of their own businesses and exuded entrepreneurial spirit. In East End terms, they knew how to make a pound note.

As a child I spent many weekends and school holidays with George, who was not only an amazing granddad, but also the most famous Pearly King in the East End. From the age of three, I would wear the pearly suit made for me by Sadie, who only had one functioning arm due to an earlier stroke, and I would help my grandfather and my other family members to raise money for charity. George would play the accordion and I would tap-dance at his side, the grand finale being the bucket shake to raise cash for the East End's needy. Being a charity fundraiser from such a young age meant I was always clear on the importance of helping others that are either less fortunate or who are affected by illness or circumstances beyond their control. I always vowed that if I ever had children they too would be introduced to the importance of giving to charity from a young age, just like I was.

When I wasn't with George, I would spend summers with Nettie at her house by the seaside. Over the course of a couple of years, she helped to undo the damage caused by the ineffective schooling I experienced in my early years. We would often sit and read pages of the dictionary or practise my writing. I would also spend time in her extensive storeroom in the West End where there were thousands of books destined for her stalls in the market. I soon became an avid reader, quickly catching up with the other children, if not surpassing them, in terms of my reading and education.

Despite times being a little tough at home, my grandparents were in fact teaching me a number of valuable life lessons and supplementing my formal education in the process. I welcomed the time with them because once I was back at home, life was all about our survival and work.

From the age of eight I used to finish school and make my own way to the print factory where my mum worked as a secretary. Luckily, my school backed on to the factory car park so it wasn't far for me to go. I used to climb through a hole in the fence in order to get there, then I would sit and wait for her to finish work at 5pm.

While I waited for her I would write stories on the clunky old typewriters or I would sit on the work bench and help collate pages and pages of order books that were then glued together before being shipped out to large companies. The smell of the print, the big machines and the paper guillotines fascinated me.

The gentlemen printers and factory workers who worked there regarded me as one of their family, and they would spend time teaching me about the various processes in the print factory while my mum finished her work. I have very fond memories of that place and the feeling of being part of something, and I felt like I had about 10 other dads who would jump in and protect my mum and me should we ever need it.

When she finished work at the printers at 5pm we would make our way to a variety of cleaning jobs, usually large betting shops and offices. We would often finish our cleaning rota at 10pm. Given our extensive working schedule, there was very little time for me to study or complete my homework. Most of the time after a 14-hour day we would just fall into bed exhausted. Every morning started with chaos as we scrambled to get ourselves ready for the next day. We would often be late for school and work as we were never prepared due to lack of time and sleep.

My dream was that one day we would be in a position to give up cleaning. I hated our routine with a passion. I could never play out after school, clubs were a no-no for a number of reasons and I was missing out on being with my friends and building important relationships because I was always working with my mum. Once I reached 11, I was old enough (in those days) to work after school and weekends. Although this meant there were occasions where mum had to clean on her own, the plus point was we were both earning and due to my additional job, I was able to contribute an extra £19 towards our household budget each week.

My weekly schedule, aged 11, was school by day, cleaning with my mum Mondays to Wednesdays from 5pm to 10pm, Thursdays I would work from 4pm to 8pm in the local pie and mash shop, Fridays I would clean our house from top to bottom, Saturdays I would work in the pie and mash shop and on Sunday I would do the weekend cleaning jobs to give my mum a break, often roping in a friend or two to help me.

If we didn't work, we didn't eat and the bills didn't get paid, it was as simple as that. I grew up knowing that if you want things in life, you have to work for them. I didn't mind working to help my mum, but there were times when I would revert to my child's view of 'life is not fair'.

I once received a letter from school stating that my year had the opportunity to go on an educational trip to Spain. The cost of the trip was £300 and I begged my mum to let me go as all the other kids were going. She told me she couldn't afford it, stating that £300 was half of our monthly earnings, and if I went we would have no money whatsoever to pay our rent or bills. Like any child at that age who doesn't understand the bigger picture, I screamed and shouted and told her it was her fault we were poor, adding that if she hadn't driven my dad away or if she had a better job we wouldn't be in this situation. As I stomped up the stairs like the teenager I was becoming, I could hear her sobbing. She hadn't wished our situation on either of us. We were where we were, and she was doing her best with the limited resources she had to make the best of a bad set of circumstances. I think I cried more than she had when my mood wore off and I realised how unreasonable I had been to expect us to be able to afford the trip in the first place. I told her that one day when I had a full-time job we would be able to go to Spain together. We just needed to get through the next five years somehow.

One of my other vivid memories is of one of the betting shops we used to clean on the corner by Shoreditch Church in London. It was a dank, dark place that stank of cigarettes and stale alcohol. Our job was to sweep up the old betting tickets and then mop the floors using an industrial-sized bucket that was bigger than I was.

Once we were finished for the night, I would stand at the bus stop with my mum and look up at the bright lights and large buildings around Liverpool Street that made up London's financial district. I dreamed of working there and earning enough money to get my mum and me out of our no-win situation and constant ritual of working and cleaning. The building I used to gaze at was the tallest building in the City at that time and the very one I could also see from my bedroom window. It stood there proud, lighting up the sky with its gleaming glass and aura of status. I knew that if I could just get a job there, things would be different. Little did I know that my first job in the City would be on the 12th floor of that exact building.

FIVE YEARS AND COUNTING

By the time I got to secondary school, I had been to three primary schools and moved home twice. When I turned up on my first day I was probably the one child that most of the kids already knew as I had either gone to their primary school or lived on their estate at some point.

Our school was a cultural melting pot given its position in the East End. I thrived in this environment as I had grown up with that kind of diversity my whole life with multiple ethnic and religious backgrounds all around me. Our maisonette was situated almost like the centre pin of a world map. Our immediate area was very much occupied by Africans and Caribbeans. Just a mile north were the Turkish, Greek and Kurdish communities, and if you went east towards Liverpool Street you'd find all of the various Asian groups. It was an amazing place to learn about the wider world, although at the time I never thought I would ever get the opportunity to visit any of those countries or experience those cultures first hand.

When I arrived at secondary school I was placed straight into the top sets for all my classes, which was probably attributable to the time I had spent learning from my mum and grandmother over the years. Even though I enjoyed my first term, I saw my time at school as a necessary evil that was preventing me from earning the money we needed. I never let dreams of college and university enter my head as I didn't want to do anything that meant our lives would have continued on with the same level of struggle as the past seven years.

Most of the kids I interacted with at school were from single-parent backgrounds, so despite our individual differences we were all bonded by our experiences of hardship in some form. In hindsight, we may not have had the best of everything, but we all learned survival instincts and extensive life skills, probably way beyond our years. For me personally, through my home life I had gained the ability to solve problems without money and to be creative with the few resources I had. I also became exceptionally streetwise and those were skills that no university later in life could have taught me. Given my background and experience, I was always going to approach problems and situations differently from say the individuals that came from the same universities and studied the same course. Even then I knew that I would never be a group thinker, more of a free thinker who would propose a mad idea on the basis that it might just work! Nowadays, especially in the workplace, this diversity of thought and innovative approach is welcomed.

Even though school was a relatively harmonious place, where I lived was a different story. My mum would do her best to help me keep up with the Joneses in terms of the clothes I wore outside school, but given our income, it was a tall order. Acceptance when you are a teenager is very much visually-based, so when I wasn't in my school uniform no one cared if I had a great personality, it was only about what Sergio tracksuit or Reebok trainers I had on. My wardrobe mostly consisted of market or charity shop finds, and I only really got kitted out when the one-parent vouchers arrived for my school uniform or my dad would buy me new clothes for Christmas.

The boys I hung around with on my estate would constantly run me down about the clothes I wore; kids can be extremely cruel. The fact that my mum had no concept of matching colours didn't help either (think red, green and yellow, with the odd brown thrown in for good measure). I often looked like I had run through my wardrobe in treacle and wore whatever stuck to me.

Out of the 13 kids I hung out with on our estate, only three had the full set of parents. The rest were brought up with stepfathers or were raised by one parent. Like any pack, you have leaders and followers, and I was at the lower end of this pack of kids with no siblings or present father figure to protect me. I was an easy target for the boys in our group to bully. As a family we were deemed to be poor, even by council estate standards. I was fairly podgy with Bugs Bunny teeth and charity shop clothes. Couple that with a fairly eccentric mother and the bullies had enough material to last them for years. Unfortunately it did go on for years.

I remember one year on Guy Fawkes night when the boys on my estate thought it would be funny to put live fireworks through our letter box. There was a screeching noise as my mum and I cowered behind the sofa as our hallway filled up with smoke. They would also shout taunts at my mum on her way home from work, throw stones up at our windows and give us prank phone calls often throughout the night. There were times when it was relentless and I truly believed it would never end. I used to wish for the winter to come as I knew at least half of them would be indoors due to the cold and they would leave us alone.

It saddens me that even today, bullying is still so rife, especially when you read about kids taking their own lives when they can't see a way to make it stop. In my day we didn't have the additional burden of bullying via social media, so for those of us at the hands of the bullies, it was all pretty much hands-on. Having been in that situation for many years, I understand how it can feel like the problem is insurmountable, but you do get through it and the key is to seek help and not to suffer in silence.

By the time I was 13, I was getting frustrated with school. I would often play truant, miss lessons and turn up late. I became a law unto myself.

All through my 'rocky period' at school, I was going to local nightclubs, smoking, drinking and experimenting with all sorts of things, often being caught by my cousins who would run back to tell my dad. He would reprimand me. To be honest, although he was an important part of my life he wasn't in it full time, so like most kids that age I would make the right noises about being sorry and carry on getting up to no good. Getting up to such antics at such a young age was relatively acceptable where I came from and it became a regular occurrence for my friends and me. We got into all sorts of trouble, but we were streetwise enough to get ourselves out of it and avoid our parents finding out what we'd been up to.

My mum did the best she could to keep me on the right track, but I was clearly at 'that age'. I told her: "You can't treat me like an adult all these years and then treat me like a child when it suits you." She would put me on the school bus, knowing I would get off at the next stop. I would get off and there she was, waiting to put me back on again. I even got caught skipping school by my dad. I was playing with my friends and I ran across the road into the path of an oncoming car, not knowing who was driving. I gave the driver a tirade of abuse and various rude hand signals before looking a little closer and realising who was behind the wheel. Of all the cars, in all the streets, it had to be my dad! Needless to say, I was ushered back to school with a strong telling-off, and when I tried to leave again via the back exit, there he was waiting to make me go back in. On reflection, I am not proud of those years and had I not had the support of a few people to get me back on track, I could have very easily taken a very different path in life.

I was removed from the majority of my school lessons, either for being too quick with my tongue or because I was the class clown. Running up and down the school hallways with the science skeleton dressed in my PE kit did not go down well with my head of year or form tutor, nor did peeling oranges all over the desk of a teacher who had a severe allergy to the fruit. My English teacher called me aside one day after lessons. She looked up at me and said: "If you don't pull your socks up, all you'll be good for is canning sardines in a factory. It's a shame, Vanessa, as I truly believe you have a lot of potential. You need to sort yourself out and stop playing around. You probably have two more years here, and then you are out into the big wide world. Without an education none of these big dreams you talk about will ever come to fruition."

Despite a few nonchalant nods and mentally rolling my eyes at the time, I left school that day thinking long and hard about what she had said. The way I saw it, I had two roads to choose from: one was made of a lot of catching up and knuckling down at school, or the other was a life of scraping by on benefits where I wouldn't be able to get a job or give my mum and me the life I had always promised.

My English teacher's talk that day gave me the kick up the backside I needed and turned out to be the reality check that put me back on track. It didn't take me long to recognise which path I wanted to take and to start reapplying myself at school. At just 15, I put my head down and put in extra hours, asking for others to help me. This caught the attention of some of my teachers, and they then rallied around me to help me catch up with my coursework and prepare for my GCSE exams.

I was lucky enough to be taken under the wing of the head of maths, a subject I clearly had an aptitude for when I wasn't playing about. There was a new program called 'L' that involved solving mathematical problems via a computer game. Completing those modules would also count towards my maths GCSE. We were one of the first schools to get computers and take GCSEs. I quickly became acquainted with this new technology and became a bit of an expert, much to the surprise of my teachers. Every spare moment I had was spent with my head of maths, playing this simulated game, solving maths problems and retrieving keys to move on to the next stage. I loved the feeling of achievement, solving problems and being rewarded. I would bury myself in 'L' in every IT class I attended until I conquered the program. At just 15 I became the highest achiever in maths in the school, a complete turnaround from where I had been just a year before.

Although I had got my act together at school, things were still tough at home. Over time, I had become everything to my mum: I was her friend, her confidant, her mother, her sister, and any number of other roles. It was a mentally draining position for a teenager to be in. I never had the luxury of being shielded from any of our problems. If we were in debt, I knew about it. If they were threatening to take our house away, I knew about it. Her problems were my problems and this included her relationship issues. I spent years as a child thinking if she just met the right man, the burden would be shared with another adult and we might even get to a point where we had an element of stability. She did eventually meet someone, however it was by no means the fairytale dream we had both hoped for; in fact it was very much the contrary.

The lack of a second income in our household and the pressure that my mother was under in order for us to pay the bills and eat was immense. There were often weeks where we would have less than £3 to live on. It seems hard to believe those times existed and I honestly don't know how we got through it, but somehow we did.

Despite everything we went through and as painful and difficult as it was at the time, it was those times that gave us an amazing amount of inner strength and resilience. When every day is a mountain, you become a fairly good climber. It was this very experience that made both my mum and me the people we went on to be, and neither of us would go back and change a thing.

As I headed towards my mid-teenage years I began to realise that the tower of strength I looked up to, my mother, was in fact being chipped away by all the difficulties she had endured during her own life. From losing her own father at 11, to renouncing her own Jewish upbringing and marrying so young, to bringing me up on her own, was starting to take its toll. Her bouts of depression were becoming more frequent. Our dire financial situation and lack of support from our closest family members were just exacerbating the situation further. It was becoming make or break for her, which would have meant make or break for me too.

The only way to prevent our downward cycle from becoming worse was for me to take total control of both our lives and give my mum the mental and financial break she so desperately needed. I felt that she had sacrificed so much to get me that far in life, so even though I was just 15, it was my turn. All I had to do was finish school, find a job and the rest, I believed, would be down to a little bit of cockney luck and a lot of hard work.

THE CLIMB

I left secondary school in 1988. At age 15¾, I literally got the bus from the East End of London and headed over to the City with 15p and a bag full of ambition. In a cheap second-hand suit and a few rough edges, I set out determined to find my fortune. What better place to start looking for it than right in the heart of the world's most amazing and successful financial district? For me, I felt like a character from my favourite film, 'The Wizard of Oz'. I was Dorothy as she stood at the foot of the yellow brick road, destined to find the Emerald City.

For the next week or so, I visited every bank in London's Square Mile, picking up countless application forms. At the end of every day after our cleaning routine, I would fill in the forms and return them by hand the next day. What I was missing in terms of academic qualifications I made up for with my written sales pitch about being hard-working, passionate and determined to succeed. After numerous rejections I was finally offered a place in one of the major banks, working in that very building I had dreamed of working in for so many years. Best of all, with my new £7,500 salary, we could finally give up the cleaning jobs for good.

I will never forget telling my dad about my new job in a bank. He was so proud of me. He said I would be the first one in the family to work in a bank and not consider robbing it – his idea of humour! He took me straight to the high street and bought me my first-ever suit from a real shop - called Tammy Girl. Skirt to the knee, fitted jacket, navy blue and sensible shoes – always sensible shoes with my dad! I didn't care about the shoes, I was just overjoyed about having a new suit and one that had never actually been worn by someone else before.

I remember my first day as a City worker so well. This time I was taking the bus with a purpose. I wasn't begging for chances. I had a real job. I was a part of the hustle and bustle of the City commuters, dashing and weaving in between each other in their quest to start their important days. Carrying my briefcase, strutting around in my new suit, I couldn't help but feel on top of the world. Less than two years before, I was the girl who was destined for a sardine factory and now here I was, a City worker, a high-flyer, and perhaps even a future banker.

I was beaming from ear to ear in the lift as we went to the 30th floor of the building. As my ears popped I noted that I was in a lift that actually worked and didn't smell of pee.

I became a telex administrator, working in a room where thousands of telexes and trade instructions were being sent through from all the banks all over the world via Swift. It was a hive of activity that now seems hard to imagine. These instructions were piled into tubes and sent through a system that used air and suction to deliver them to all the different departments all over the bank. I was fascinated by the sea of printing machines and the tippity-tap of the global telexes. I was at the centre of it all in some sort of mad mission control, and I couldn't have been happier.

I wasn't the only one to join the bank that day, and I quickly made friends with two other new girls who also came from diverse backgrounds. We were outsiders by comparison with the rest of the intake, which was full of university graduates and college students, mostly from privileged backgrounds. The group that was training us as part of our induction was from the intake of the previous year and their network was well formed, whereas we three just had each other.

The self-appointed leader of the group that was training us was a tall dark-haired girl who I'll call Emma. Emma was very beautiful and intelligent, but many feared her. It soon became evident that everyone around her knew their place, which was undoubtedly beneath her! Emma was the best-dressed girl on the floor and of course went out with the best-looking guy. She was popular with all the bank's managers and ensured we all knew it. She ran the show, she was the queen bee and we were just her mere workers. She was often rude to me and my two colleagues, and I guess I knew from day one that my interactions with her wouldn't end well. That said, I knew that bowing to her would be a necessary evil if I wanted to do well in my role, and I made every effort to impress her with my work. Each attempt failed miserably. She had her favourites and I clearly wasn't one of them. By way of association, my two colleagues were generally ostracised by her too. She purposely left me out of social gatherings or would talk over the top of me or dismiss my opinion and ridicule me in an open forum. She also made countless comments about one of my colleagues' weight and would ask silly questions about the other's ethnic background, which annoyed me even more. Neither of my friends would stick up for themselves when this happened. I was so disappointed, as I really thought bullies wouldn't exist in the grown-up world. I was determined not to stoop to her level, but deep down I knew it would only be a matter of time before she would eventually get the better of me.

Where I come from we tend to settle disputes extremely openly and verbally, and we stick up for our own. There was none of this sly and underhand way of digging at someone. If we had something to say we said it. If we didn't like someone we made it clear, and there would be a silent agreement to stay out of each other's way. This world of insidious corporate backstabbing was completely new territory for me and I didn't know quite how to deal with it. With no one to turn to in the bank for help, or other supporters with corporate experience to seek advice from, I just dealt with each situation the only way I knew how.

I only managed to keep my composure for four months. Over lunch one day as I listened to her drop less than subtle comments about my background, my friend's weight and the other's ethnicity, I just snapped. As my friends and I got up to leave the table, I heard her say to her colleagues, "I don't know why we take these council rejects in the first place."

As I looked back at her, I could see her cackling expression; just like the Wicked Witch of the West, it was like she was saying to me, "I'll get you my pretty, and your little dogs too", her eyes penetrated me as she cackled. Months of her goading me was finally going to yield the response she desired, I was lost for any kind of words that would have portrayed my anger and upset, so I retaliated, in probably what was the worst way possible. I threw what was left of my salad over her. I hadn't planned it, my arm moved before my 16-year-old brain could tell it to stop, and the moment I had done it, I regretted it. Before I knew it, she and I were locked nose to nose in confrontation in front of the entire cafeteria.

When I got back to my desk, I was summoned to the head of department's office. The bank's managers then locked me in a room for two hours to interrogate me for my actions in the canteen. By now, Emma and her closest friends had accused me of all sorts. When I reflect on the situation now with all my HR experience, I cannot believe how badly it was handled. I recall my mother coming up to the bank to sit with me through their interview process, and they locked her in the interrogation room too!

I explained to the head of department exactly what had been going on over the past few months and gave him names of people who could corroborate my side of the story. He had already clearly made up his mind about who was to blame and, let's face it, it was my lack of control that caused the situation to escalate when I should have just walked away.

I was placed on gardening leave for one week while they continued to investigate. Needless to say, they didn't do the same to Emma as she had an impeccable record, and from what I heard afterwards they felt that this would damage her future career.

I was summoned back to the bank and they offered to reinstate me, albeit in a branch in Leicester which was 150 miles from where I lived! I got the hint and submitted my resignation. I had lost complete faith in the place as I felt they hadn't dealt with the situation fairly; yes I was wrong, but there were two sides to the story and mine had clearly been lost. I chose to leave as I knew this was one battle I wasn't going to win. I also learned an important lesson about self-control and fighting other people's battles, as neither of my two colleagues stood by me during the investigation even though they were the actual victims of her bullying too.

I sulked for a day or two in a haze of 'life's not fair', and then off I went again, knapsack on my back, to find another job as I contemplated the lessons about self-control and how there would be people I would meet during my corporate journey who would push my boundaries. I vowed I would never get into that situation again.

I had been totally put off banking for the time being and decided to pursue my other passion, which was IT. My IT exam result was actually an F grade since I had spent all of my IT lesson time focusing on my maths exam, so securing a pure IT role was going to be hard. But when had I ever taken the easy route?

My plan was to try and find a decent job in an IT firm, then work my way up and perhaps move back to a bank later on in my career. I took a few temp roles as an office junior to get by, but my main intent was still to work in IT. During my stay as a temp receptionist at a venture capital firm, I had the opportunity to work with a woman called Marley who really took me under her wing and restored my faith in people in the workplace.

During our quiet times, she would teach me about her role as a secretary and I utilised my spare time learning to type properly. I was a self-taught typist from the age of seven having played on the typewriters and typesetters at my mum's printing company job, but my fingers were all over the place so I wasn't as fast as I could have been. Back in those days a typing test was standard practice to get any form of secretarial job. Marley bought me a Pitman's book of typing lessons and used to help me sit there and practise. Every afternoon and every lunchtime I would open my book and raise my fingers on to the keyboard ASDF: LKJ – over and over again for hours.

When the temp assignment ended because the company was closing down, not only had I learned everything there was to know about being a secretary thanks to Marley, I was now also a 70-word-per-minute typist! That temp job was time well spent and proof that putting in the effort can reap rewards.

After weeks of scanning the national papers looking for that golden IT opportunity, I was starting to think that I was destined to be a temp forever, flitting from one job to another with no real destination. The week before my firm was due to close I was at the end of a rain-soaked journey on the No. 38 bus when I happened to pick up a crumpled local newspaper left on the seat beside me. I opened the first page and there it was: 'Receptionist wanted for IT firm'. For once, I was in the right place at the right time and fate had played its hand.

I managed to secure that receptionist role at the IT firm mostly by using my wit and charm at the interview. I told the two suave MDs that sat before me that I would work really hard, and not only would I do the job they hired me for, but I could also double up as a secretary. All they had to do was give me a chance. I think I might have also offered to clean the offices after work if they gave me the role, something they thankfully never took me up on. Needless to say, I got the position, and once again the jumping for joy began. I was back in the game.

The company sold IT equipment and training services in an industry that was clearly booming. From the moment I arrived I loved it there – a small organisation where everyone knew everyone else, and the great thing was that it was a firm that was clearly growing. You could smell the ambition from the sales team, and the buzz of the procurement team as vanloads of shiny new IT kit left, destined for large companies.

I really enjoyed my role as the company's first line of contact with our customers. I did everything to ensure that my reception desk, call answering and customer service was everything it could possibly be. After six months on reception, I started to help out the training team, mostly binding manuals and creating delegate registers in my quiet periods at first, but I knew that training really interested me as did the whole concept of teaching others.

After sharing my enthusiasm and many offers to help, I was offered a transfer into the training department as a training administrator. My role was to meet and greet candidates before their training courses started, look after the training rooms, manage the public schedule, type up confirmation letters and, if I did well, I could start to manage our pool of external trainers. I made sure it went well, and little by little as I shadowed my manager I started to think I could actually become a training manager or trainer myself one day.

I came in one Monday and was called into the office by the MD. Both MDs were fairly scary (to a 17-year-old anyway), and I couldn't quite imagine what they would want with me. My first thought was what have I done wrong? All I had done since I started was keep my head down, work hard and stay out of trouble. He sat me down and said: "Look, your boss needs some time out of the office. She will probably be gone for a good four to eight weeks. You are going to have to run the department and keep it on track while she is away. We will keep our eye on you, but basically it's your ship." I felt worried for my boss because they never really explained why she needed time away, but I was excited at the same time. I was being given the opportunity to step up and really show what I was made of, and I did.

Over the next two months, I took responsibility for all the

processes end-to-end. The sales team were bringing in the sales, and the operational side was running like clockwork. They even let me hire an administrator to help me. The department was thriving. We were bringing in new clients, making more money than we had in the last year and were making fewer mistakes than ever. I started to realise how organised I was and that I actually had a talent for working with people and sales. Above all, I realised that I excelled under pressure.

My boss was due back in less than three weeks, and once again I was pulled aside by the MD. "Vanessa, you are doing such a good job that when your boss returns we may actually move her into another role or get rid of her altogether. We were thinking that you could continue running the team, but as their manager." Despite being overjoyed at the prospect of the promotion, I couldn't help but feel that what he was offering me was wrong. How could he be so backhanded? My boss had worked her guts out to build our department from scratch. I had held the department together for my boss and the firm to prove what I was capable of, not to do her out of a job! I felt disappointed and conflicted. I didn't want to seem ungrateful, but at the same time my value system was telling me that getting ahead as a consequence of someone else's unfair downfall was wrong.

I had heard on the grapevine through a couple of the trainers that there was a training manager role going at one of the major publishing houses. Despite loving where I worked, I decided to go for the role and a few others to see if I could secure a similar promotion somewhere else. I desperately didn't want to go back to binding manuals and looking after the training rooms when my boss eventually returned. I figured that if I could get another job elsewhere, I could hand back the department to my boss in great working order, she could continue in the role she clearly loved, and I would take the next logical step in my career. All sorted, everyone is a winner, or so I thought.

I got the job at the publishing house, and a couple of days after she returned to the office I nervously called my boss into a meeting room to hand in my resignation. I had no intention of telling her about the conversation I'd had with our MDs. My plan was to tell her I had learned so much from her and having had the experience of running the department myself for a couple of months, I now felt I was able to move on and try to do the same role elsewhere. Her department was now doing really well, and in terms of what I was leaving behind there were formidable sales in the pipeline and a number of new clients already signed on. Rather than being understanding as I expected, her reaction probably put me off working for women for the next five years!!

As I handed her my letter, her face became solemn and she began to wail at me like a banshee. "How could you leave me? Is it because you're not up for the job? Are you leaving to cover all the mistakes you have made?" and so on. She was throwing her hands in the air and leaning over the table into my personal space and shouting at me so close I could feel her breath. My blood pressure went up because she was actually scaring me, and I knew that I was in one of those fight-or-flight moments. I thought, paused and breathed, reflecting on the lessons learnt from the salad incident. Despite desperately wanting to tell her that I had actually saved her job and spent the last three months keeping it all together, working 15-hour days and growing the training side of the business for her to return to, I simply stood up and said: "I am really sorry you feel that way, but my decision is final." Less was definitely more in that particular situation. I walked back to my desk, completely choked that after all I had done it had still managed to go wrong.

I started the job at the publishing house. My role was to manage the training budget and organise a programme that would see all 300 employees fully trained in Microsoft and cc:Mail. About six months into the programme, one of my external trainers called in sick. Rather than cancel the course, I thought this would be an ideal opportunity to try and teach it myself. I had sat in on a number of previous courses and I knew the system inside out, so why not? I asked my boss if this was an option and he told me to go for it, with a warning that if it went well he would expect me to run all of the intro mail courses and save money from the training budget. It did go well, and before I knew it, I was not only running the programme but training internal delegates two days a week. I branched out from cc:Mail, invested in a few train-the-trainer days from the money I had saved, and before I knew it I was training Microsoft Office at an intro level across the firm. I was the golden girl, adding value, saving money and also acting as a small support function for the IT team.

Life was rosy. As a family, we weren't cleaning anymore and above all I had a suit for each day of the week. My mum had managed to get a better job in a housing association and was earning a bit more money. Between us we were also managing to clear her debt. I was now a manager at the tender age of 22. I had my own car and had even managed to get my own little flat in a low-rise council block in Hoxton, ironically where life had started all those years ago. I couldn't see the City buildings anymore, but I didn't have to. I worked in one of those buildings and my dreams as a little girl were actually starting to come to fruition.

My programme of training at the publishing house was actually running two months ahead of schedule and was under budget due to the amount of doubling up I was doing in my role. Sadly, the publishing house had hit hard times as the internet came along, and it was only a matter of time before they were going to start making redundancies.

I remember looking around my department and thinking that perhaps if I offered myself up I could save those people who would be badly hit by being made redundant – those people with families and mortgages and real responsibilities. I was only young – would it really matter if I left? I had learned so much, and maybe it was time to move on and use the redundancy money to set up my own small business as a freelance trainer. I had all the contacts, I knew a number of external firms held me in high regard and I knew getting work wasn't going to be a problem. It was a risk, but my theory was that if it all went wrong, I would just dust myself off and look for another job.

My boss was quite shocked when I put my proposal to him, but I told him it was what I wanted to do and convinced him that this was win/win. I would be the sacrificial lamb as my role wouldn't really exist once the training programme finished and he could hold on to the other resources he needed. Not only did they make me redundant and look after me above and beyond financially, they also realised that with me leaving there was still an element of my training programme that needed to be completed. Much to my surprise, they then hired me back for three months as a contractor, which alongside my redundancy payment enabled me to set aside enough money to start my own training business, with a few months' leeway if the work dried up.

Capitalising on my contacts in the training industry, my fledgling business went from strength to strength. I was MD of my own company at just 22 and my skills were massively in demand, even for packages I didn't know how to teach, because they wanted my style of delivery. This meant that the majority of my evenings were spent learning new applications, whilst most of my mates were out having fun. At one point I was able to train over 22 different packages to an intermediate/ advanced level. I had also started consulting, putting together large training needs analysis programmes for big corporations and their intern programmes.

I was now earning approximately £1,250 per week, sometimes more. Earning that sort of money was more than enough to start to give me and my mum a bit of the good life and clear her debt once and for all. I upgraded my beaten-up old Mini to a shiny old-style BMW and my suits and shoes got a tad more expensive too. It was the first time in our lives that we didn't have to worry about money. After 22 years of climbing our way out of debt, I can't explain how good it felt to be able to answer the front door without the fear of the person on the other side threatening to take away our TV and sofa.

After a year of living the high life I received my first tax bill from the Inland Revenue. Being so young, I hadn't quite got my head around the tax system, nor had I put anything away from my weekly earnings. I didn't even have an accountant! I then realised that there was a side to business I didn't like: paperwork, VAT returns, tax returns, keeping umpteen receipts, and above all paying others my hard-earned cash when I couldn't see the value they added. I decided at this point that it might be an idea to go permanent at one of the firms I had been consulting for and shut my company down. I had been working five days a week and studying in the evenings, and had slowly come to realise that the business was in fact just me and I had spent the last nine months flogging that particular asset to death. I needed a bit of financial stability and I wanted to ensure that all my tax affairs were being taken care of for me. First rule of business, always pay the tax man. I wish someone had been around to tell me that one! I also appreciated that if I was going to set up my own business in the future there was more that I needed to learn. That would take time, and it was time I didn't have at that point.

I joined a big consulting firm I had previously been working for which had a solid pipeline of work providing training programmes to large corporations. I loved having paid leave again and the odd day off. The only problem with this job was the travelling. They would send me all over the country to train, so for two years I lived like a nomad and often out of a bag. They would also expect me to be able to learn a package the day before and teach it the next day. I always managed to pull it off, more due to the fact that I would stay up all night to learn it well so as not to let them down. Looking back on it, it was an unfair position to be put in and I wish I could have been a little stronger and pushed back on some of their demands.

Slowly but surely, I was becoming one of their top trainers. Companies would specifically request me to run their courses and I rarely got less than a 10/10 as a performance score from all my delegates. In spite of my confident demeanour, however, I was still battling with numerous insecurities that stemmed from my background, especially my cockney accent.

Whenever I had to train graduates, I would do my best to put on my poshest speaking voice as I felt awkward about my own accent. For some reason I had this ridiculous notion that they would judge me or perceive that I was not worthy to teach them if I spoke in my normal voice.

These graduates were brought in as part of the grad or internship programmes by some of the top banks and consultancies. They arrived after having been courted from their universities, wined and dined and flown all over the world. Their companies would basically blow a huge amount of smoke up their backsides about what they would one day become and be earning. What they didn't know is that once they got into their jobs they probably wouldn't see the light of day for around five years as they would be travelling extensively. Even after a good 10 years of service their chances of making partner or MD was limited, only the golden few got through (and very few of them were women).

Our job as trainers was to make them technologically proficient. There were many courses where my palms would be sweaty and my heart would be racing as I dreaded teaching them. I was so convinced that the moment I opened my mouth, or if my grammar slipped in some way, they would lose respect for me. I'm sure the problem was more about my own insecurities than anything else as not once did any of my delegates make me feel this way. It wasn't until later on in my career that I faced such prejudice.

I trained for that company for a couple of years before moving on to another training consultancy I had dealt with back in my days at the publishing house. The work was much the same, and once again I was living out of a bag as I began to travel to Europe too.

Holding down relationships was always a problem given the extensive amount of travelling my job entailed. Most of my partners got bored of never seeing me and a fair few didn't understand my ambition either. In one particular relationship, the more successful I became, the more he didn't like it. I was never going to let myself get into a controlling relationship like that, where I was made to feel bad about my ambitions, after seeing what my mum had gone through. Despite many of my relationships ending and the fact it hurt at the time, my heart healed fast as I was focused on my bigger goals around career success.

I had now become a senior trainer within my firm and was offered the chance to go and work on a long-term training programme at a large pharmaceutical company. Our role was to train over 3,000 people globally on their new IT build and its customised applications. My role would also be leading teams of trainers, often travelling to global locations to train in the company's regional offices.

My grandmother, Nettie had just passed away after a second bout of breast cancer which left me devastated. In some ways she was as much of a mum to me as my own. She had left me some money in her will with a caveat that I should invest it wisely. I knew exactly what she meant and I decided to invest it in my first property which I bought in one of the home counties near London. I wasn't going to let her down.

I would be working in the nearby area anyway so it made perfect sense. I purchased my three-bed semi, falling for style over substance. I actually ended up with the best house in the worst possible street, but it didn't matter. I had lived in worse places, and the bottom line was that I had a house I owned which was still an achievement for someone who was only 23.

Moving away from my flat in London was a big move. I was with a partner I knew couldn't afford the cost of the new commute, so that was undoubtedly going to end yet another relationship. From a personal perspective the City high life with its partying and endless drinking sessions had started to take its toll. I worked hard but I played harder, it was the motto of the 1990s! Some of my colleagues were only just discovering in their twenties what I had been doing for the best part of seven years going out in the City. On reflection, I was probably on the edge of burning out. Upping sticks and moving away was the perfect escape, even if it meant moving away from all the things that made me feel secure, like my friends and above all my mum.

Once again, living out of a bag became the norm. During this time my relationship did fizzle out and I became friends with Stewart, one of the IT engineers who was also on site for a third party company. I liked his shyness and his intelligence, and above all he made me laugh. He wasn't naturally my type. I had always thought, given my previous relationships, that I would end up as a gangster's moll or with a City wide boy, not with a normal bloke who had a normal job.

Every morning before my training course would start, I would pull the leads out of the back of my computer and log a helpdesk call so he would come to my classroom to fix my PCs. He said nothing, he would just fix what he knew was an engineered fault on my part and make his way back to his desk, only to see another call logged in my name later that day. After waiting three weeks for him to make his move, I sent him an email one afternoon saying: Aren't I the brave one? and our relationship started from there. Within four months, I found us having a conversation at an airport gate where he said to me that he could not continue to drop me off at airports because he missed me too much. I actually missed him too, and I wasn't enjoying travelling around the world either. Living in hotel rooms and spending copious amounts of time in airports or cabs is not as glamorous as people might think.

If there was ever going to be any future to our relationship I knew I needed to put my passport away for a while, settle down and give our relationship a go.

Given my growing interest in the technical side of IT, I knew I could find another job in the world of technical support which would also allow me to stop travelling.

My CV was quite long already and getting jobs had become easier with all the experience I had gained over the years. I managed to find a local job which was 30 minutes from home and £5k more than I had been earning. There was only one issue clouding my excitement: the role was reporting to a woman and I still bore the scars of my previous encounters with female bosses. It almost put me off taking the role.

The firm I was still working for was now headed by one of the first managing directors I'd worked for back in my days as a receptionist. I was one of their best trainers and they were not going to let me go without a fight. Despite my best efforts, they held me to a three-month resignation period, making me travel to all sorts of far-off destinations and undertaking the worst of the training schedule. They were clearly intent on getting their pound of flesh before I left. I would be in one part of the country one day and have to travel overnight to the next. I tried to negotiate with them and told them that the boss of my new company was pressuring me to start within two months, but they wouldn't budge. The MD hadn't changed his spots from the previous time I worked for him.

During my resignation period, Stewart moved in. I was still travelling extensively and my last assignment before I finished was in Philadelphia. I had asked Stewart to come and join me for a week's holiday in New York to celebrate my new job and our new beginning. It was there on top of the Empire State Building that Stewart got down on one knee in front of 50 or so tourists and asked me to marry him. After giving him a lecture about marriage being just a piece of paper and reminding him that the divorce rate in my family was 98%, I eventually said yes. We set the date to get married for the following year.

I left the training company and joined a large insurer, working as a desktop support analyst for a small team under my female boss who actually turned out to be one of the best bosses I have ever had. Six months later Stewart left his role as an IT engineer and joined the same firm in a similar role to mine but in a different department.

It was only then that I started to notice the difference between the girls' and the boys' club. My future husband was educated at one of the best public schools in London, the Latymer. He had also been to university and had graduated with an impressive set of degrees. He was quickly adopted by what I called the 'red socks brigade', made up of the ex-public school boys who abound in the world of finance.

These individuals looked after each other in a myriad of ways. They furthered each other's careers, employed each other's sons and played golf together while their wives lunched. I watched Stewart's career soar under the guidance of these individuals and he was being offered roles normally taken by individuals 10 years his senior. One of his bosses even demoted one of his female direct reports and placed Stewart into her role. This type of behaviour appeared to be commonplace, and I started to understand that this was how the corporate world worked, where the rules stated that for some individuals, there were no rules!

I continued in my role to the best of my ability, learning how to dismantle PCs and printers, but despite my popularity I was relatively unnoticed career-wise. My little team were under the radar of the red socks brigade as my boss was a woman. She didn't have a club background, nor did she play golf. I watched her work tirelessly, often not getting the support she needed from the upper echelons of our firm or the recognition she deserved, but still she continued. Her love and loyalty to the job knew no bounds, and given my loyalty to her and my passion for any job I undertake, I mirrored her behaviour.

Stewart's career continued to progress at a pace. There really wasn't any major difference in terms of our skillsets or ability, but he was being championed by others and the doors of opportunity were being opened to help his career. I started to understand that being successful was not just about being present and doing your job well. It had everything to do with your connections, who you knew and who knew you. I hadn't invested in that side of my career at all. Up until then, I had been very focused and driven in my approach, thinking that my output on the printer at the end of the day was how my work was being measured and that it was that output and my ridiculous hours that would ultimately determine my next promotion and success.

I had every intention of building my career, and was feeling quite confident about mirroring my husband's opportunities and his career trajectory. I just needed to work out how to do it.

Slowly I was becoming my boss's deputy, and it was just a matter of time before an opportunity came up where I could take on a role as a tech team leader. I had even contemplated working in London again should a role come up there. There was just one tiny little unplanned spanner in the works for my next steps – I was pregnant.

AND THEN THERE WERE THREE (AND THEN FOUR)

Four tests later and the line was still bright blue. I was poking Stewart with the stick as he slept. "Stew, I'm pregnant!" I was absolutely petrified. As I lay back on my bed, looking at my open-mouthed and clearly shocked husband, I could tell we were thinking the same thing. How were we going to look after a baby when we could barely look after ourselves?

We had agreed after we had got married that if it happened, it happened. And it happened, less than six months after the wedding. To be honest, I had spent years thinking I wouldn't be able to have kids for some reason. I expect it is a fear that a lot of women have before they actually conceive.

I felt a mixture of emotions being pregnant. One part of me was ecstatic, and the other was horrified at the thought of something growing inside my body. Being an only child I had no experience of kids whatsoever. Stewart was the last of three children so he wasn't exactly an expert either. The normal fears kicked in after the first few weeks. How were we ever going to afford this baby? What would happen to my career? Would I have to give up work? Why was I bringing a new life into the world when society as a whole was in such a mess? Would I be able to handle the responsibility? Above all, would I be a good mum?

There were so many thoughts running through my mind, and I had no idea at the time that this was perfectly normal for a first-time parent.

I still didn't believe I was pregnant until I saw my scan picture and laid eyes on this little prawn-looking thing that was a consequence of Stewart and I. However, there it was, absolute proof that in six months' time we were going to be a proper family with real responsibilities. Life was about to change again.

During my pregnancy, I gained 83 pounds. If you think about this in real terms, I almost doubled in size. The weight didn't bother me initially because for once in my life I thought I had a license not to watch my weight as I was eating for two (which was probably more like eating for four).

Aside from enjoying the wonderful feeling of being pregnant, I kept thinking about what would happen in the longer term. How would we afford childcare? Would my firm be willing to let me go part time? Was it even an option? There was one thing I knew for sure – I was definitely going back to work.

My pregnancy flew by, and before I knew it I was three weeks away from my due date. I left work on a tide of support, gifts and good wishes. My boss and colleagues had been brilliant throughout my entire pregnancy, and I couldn't have wished for a greater send off.

Throughout my pregnancy I had made it abundantly clear that my intention was to come back to work. I told my boss I would be away for three to four months maximum. I suggested to her that I might need to return part-time, but once I had a routine and childcare sorted out, I would come back full time. She just smiled and said: "I will support you in whatever you want to do, but why don't you see how you feel once you have had the baby?" I think she half expected me to change my mind, which was understandable. I was full of preconceived ideas about what I would and wouldn't do as a working mum and parent, what the baby would eat, whether they would ever watch TV and how we as parents would deal with certain situations. Most of those ideas went out of the window the moment she was born. There is a lot to be said for planning and I wholly advocate it, but you can't plan for every situation. Believe me, there are many things we didn't plan for when it came to our children, such as how we were going to balance two careers and our pending bundle of joy.

I left for maternity fully expecting to have three weeks of lunches and nesting. I had been off just one week when I went into labour early. After a turbulent 24 hours involving various medical interventions my daughter was born.

As I looked at this amazing bundle of joy that Stewart and I had made, I found it difficult to comprehend she was mine. I knew I loved her because I was supposed to, but I didn't get that gush of emotion I had read about in so many maternity magazines. In fact, I felt no maternal instinct towards her whatsoever. I found giving birth almost like a job I had to do, and once it was done I expected to move on to the next job. It didn't seem to sink in that she was in fact the next job, a job I would have to do for the rest of my life. I don't know to this day if it was some form of post-natal depression, shock of childbirth or what it was, but looking back I cannot comprehend how a new mother could feel like that. However, I did, and I hated myself for it.

My daughter was quite sickly after the birth because she'd been borderline premature and she was on watch by all of the doctors. When my waters broke, my labour had not started and there had been no water in my womb to protect her for more than 14 hours. She had also swallowed her own meconium which is very dangerous for a newborn. A day after she was born, the nurse came to take her for a visit to the ward paediatrician. "I am going to take your daughter to the paediatrician, Mrs Vallely," she said. "Do you want to get dressed to accompany me?" My response was: "No, it's fine, you can just take her, I'm sure she'll be fine." Stewart was horrified, and my mum gasped. I honestly didn't see what the fuss was about at the time. "Vanessa, that's your baby!" my mum exclaimed. "I know that," I said, "but I am sure they know what they are doing." Silence fell as the nurse took my daughter away to see the paediatrician. Stewart followed her, shooting me a dark look I had never seen before.

I didn't know how to explain how I felt. Yes, I was normally a tower of strength, however this was totally new territory. I didn't feel ready for a baby, and for once I didn't know what I was doing and couldn't blag my way through. Most things I have ever tried to master I have succeeded at in some form, however being a mum just wasn't coming naturally to me; I couldn't even breastfeed her no matter how hard I tried. It had taken me the whole nine months to accept that I was even pregnant, therefore I wasn't going to take to motherhood overnight. I couldn't tell my family how I was feeling as I didn't understand it myself. If there were two words to sum up my view of myself at that moment, they were 'selfish failure', and worse still I didn't have the courage to talk to anyone about how I was feeling. All the glossy magazines and baby books were talking about glowing new mothers who were just naturally maternal, so why wasn't I feeling like that, what was wrong with me.

The nurse brought her back and when she laid my baby down in her cot, I noticed her hand was purple. "We couldn't get the needle into her hand, we had a bit of trouble," the nurse explained. I looked at Stewart and to this day I can't explain the feeling inside of me. It was like a volcano erupting in my stomach and a pain in my heart like I have never known. Even though they were making her better, they had hurt her, my little girl, and worse still I hadn't been there to protect her. If that was my maternal instinct arriving, it did so in grand style.

My eyes filled up with tears as I cradled my daughter in my arms. "What did they do to you, little girl, Mummy is so sorry," I cried. There were sighs from my mum and Stewart as they realised that the penny had finally dropped. I was her mum and she was my darling daughter. The nurse reassured me that babies bruised easily. Stewart had been with her the whole time and they just had trouble getting the needle into her tiny little hand because of how small she was. Needless to say, she never went anywhere without me by her side from that point and she never ever will.

I spent the first three months bonding with my beautiful little girl, although some of it still didn't come 100% naturally to me. I always struggled to play. I had not really played much as a child myself or, if I did, it tended to be on my own, so I actually didn't know how to play with others. I would start to play with her and then wander off into a world of my own. I joked with Stewart that I wished she had come with a manual or a process map so that I would have known what to do when she did something unexpected.

It will come as no great surprise that I wasn't a coffee morning mum. I tried my best, attending many mother and baby events with my daughter, meeting other mums and sharing stories. I enjoyed some of the interactions, but not the competitiveness of it all. When the kids were about nine months old, one mum was telling me that her son could already walk. She then basically dragged this child across the room when he clearly couldn't even put his weight on his feet. I'd seen enough.

I had kept in touch with my boss throughout my maternity leave, finding out what was going on and what the plans were for the team. Three months flew by and I couldn't wait to get back to work, even if it was only for a couple of days a week. I was very fearful that technology would have moved on and when I returned I might not have the required skills to do my job or to continue where I had left off. That said, there was this other big part of me that didn't want to leave my daughter, and I wanted the best of both worlds. Luckily they agreed for me to return three days a week, which I think was more to do with my boss campaigning for it than anything else.

The first day I dropped my daughter off at the nursery I felt like someone had removed my heart with a spoon. There she was, this tiny little bundle, just three months old and I was leaving her in the hands of a virtual stranger.

While I'd been looking forward to going back to work, I was still 55 pounds overweight and this had a big impact on my confidence. Why had I not sprung back like all the celebrity mums in the magazines? I had done my best to fit in exercise during my maternity leave and I watched what I was eating once my daughter was born, but often I would just grab the nearest thing to hand. It didn't help that I would often skip breakfast and eat late at night as I was very much fitting my needs around the baby.

I started to notice when I was overweight that people were treating me differently. I could no longer hide behind the fact I was pregnant; now I was just overweight, a UK size 20 and in the category the doctors like to call clinically obese. There is an assumption by some that when you are carrying that much weight, all you do is sit at home and eat all day. That certainly wasn't the case. It had taken me nine months to put on that much weight and I would have been a fool to think that I would have the baby and it would all just disappear. I felt I was under an incredible amount of pressure to make that happen. I recall going to a plus-size store to buy a suit to return to work in. What amazed me was the lack of choice and the fact everything I tried on made me feel bigger than I actually was. I had friends who previously complained how hard it was to find plus-sized clothes that were flattering and fashionable, but I never figured how hard until I was in this situation myself. The whole experience was upsetting and if anything made my confidence issues worse, as if you look good, you feel good. My body was a weird version of its former self, my brain felt like it had been pushed through a cheese grater and all of those demons about whether I still had what it took professionally were lurking in the back of my mind. There was a big part of me that was fairly feisty and itching to get back to work however at the same time there was this little person sitting on my shoulder wishing we could have afforded for me to stay off work a little longer.

Giving up work in any form was a pipe dream. Our salaries covered our bills with a few trimmings, but there was no way one of us could not work. I had to go back, and three days was the bare minimum we could afford. Childcare was expensive but I wanted to give my daughter the best care my money could buy. When I first left Mia at her nursery, she didn't even bat an eyelid, which made me feel even worse – had my initial non-bonding experience affected her? Had I spent enough time with her so she would remember I was her mum? There were so many emotions to deal with on top of questions like could I still do my job, would my colleagues resent me for working part time, and would being off work for a few months affect my long-term prospects? I left the nursery that first day like most new mums, in a flood of tears.

Despite only being gone for three months, I returned and the entire organisation and its management structure was completely up in the air. This was due to the fact that whilst I was away, the organisation's IT department had been outsourced to a third party IT service provider. The job I was being offered was not the same position or at the same level as the role I left. Organisations were not bound in those days to give you a similar role when you returned from maternity leave; it was on a best endeavours basis only. I don't believe it was their intention to place me in a lesser role, but that was what it was. I was a victim of organisational change and circumstance.

The role I was returning to was a back office role. Out of sight of people and of all the things I was good at. Before I had left I had worked my way up to gold technical support which meant that I was providing IT tech support to our MDs and directors, and I was just on the cusp of running my team. Now here I was, going back to a role with little opportunity for the future. I was placed in one of our oldest buildings, setting up new user accounts. Shuffling form after form, day after day, the measure of my success was how many accounts I could set up or third-line calls I could deal with in one day. It may have been a great role for someone, but that someone certainly wasn't me. I couldn't believe that this was what I had returned to work for, and I thought there absolutely had to be another way. But the prospect of leaving seemed out of the question – who would take me, a new mum who could only work part time?

I worked from 8am to 4pm, three days a week for three months, upping it to four days during the fourth month, which was more a financial decision than anything else. We needed to move house, and the only way we could do it was if we were bringing in more money. Stewart was now working in London, and thanks to his hard work and the support of the 'red socks' he was now running all of the support teams across the UK offices. I would try to interact with him about work and his career once my daughter was sleeping, but he was working hard and he was tired. I felt very much as if I was being left behind.

I coasted through my role in security admin, trying to juggle my job, being a mum and losing my remaining weight. Deep down I knew this was no time for career advancement as I couldn't put in the hours, and for once in my life I felt that the ambition had been knocked out of me. I was a new mum in a dead end job. I just had to accept that this was a period of my career that was on hold, and I needed to focus on trying to balance it all. I knew my ambition would return as would the opportunities, I just had to accept that the time would come when I could reapply myself and fulfil my career ambitions.

After a few months of becoming more and more brain dead, I knew I had to make a change for my own sanity. I heard there was a position in London working as a project analyst. It was a side step, but it was a change and a chance for me to re-engage with my career. All I had was the hiring manager's name on an org chart with a blank box next to it saying 'Vacant'. I thought long and hard before I emailed him. The job was back in London, it was possibly full time, and I knew I wanted a sibling for my daughter at some point. If I applied for the job and actually got it, how would I juggle two kids, my new career and a commute to London?

Nothing ventured, nothing gained and I emailed the hiring manager in spite of my concerns. I explained that I was a new mum who was desperate to restart her career with a new opportunity. I used the same sales pitch as I had used for so many jobs in the past. As I hit the send button, I prayed he would respond and give me a chance. I knew I didn't have the necessary experience, but once again I made it abundantly clear that I exuded passion and drive and would do whatever it took to learn in my own time.

Much to my surprise, I was invited to London to meet him to discuss the opportunity. The moment I stepped off the train at Liverpool Street, I knew I was home. By hook or by crook I was going to get back on that train later that afternoon with that job – I knew London was where I was supposed to be.

The gentleman I met was called Roy, a studious-looking man from what I assumed was a middle class background. He reminded me of Joe 90 from Thunderbirds as I could barely see his eyes through the thickness of his glasses. Behind this professorial persona was in fact one of the warmest and most genuine individuals I had ever met. Little did I know that Roy would not only provide me with a platform to relaunch my career, but he would also go on to become one of my role models and biggest advocates.

Roy took a chance on me by giving me the role. He agreed to take me on and teach me the ropes with the help of his long-term programme management office (PMO) manager, Elaine. I remember investing £50 in project management books and studying when my daughter went to bed. I was desperate to supplement my knowledge outside the office wherever and however I could. Bit by bit I began to understand the project lifecycle and my role as a project analyst.

Elaine took me under her wing, teaching me everything she knew about running a successful PMO. As a long-term employee of the new outsource firm, she was a stranger to our firm, finding her way and building her relationships. I helped her to integrate as she helped me to launch a new career. I observed how Roy and Elaine operated. They were a formidable pair who often finished each other's sentences. Normally in that kind of a situation three is a crowd, but those two welcomed me with open arms and we soon became the three amigos.

I was now in a new world of opportunity. The organisation I worked for had multiple clients and the people I worked with had worked across all of them, from insurance to oil and gas, from marketing to finance. I knew I was part of something very exciting. I was learning new things and I was building a support network. I also had balance with my home life. Once again I felt that I had an opportunity to make progress with my career.

Balancing my new career and the commute back and forth to London was another challenge – not just the reliance on the trains but ensuring I left the office at a decent time. There is nothing quite like that walk of shame when you are leaving the office early and others are not. I would tidy my desk and hang around as long as I could without missing my train. My feelings of guilt about leaving the office were very much my own because Roy and Elaine were always supportive. They knew that the eight hours I put in was worth 10 hours of someone less capable, so they allowed me to be flexible.

Stewart's hours at work were increasing as his career went from strength to strength. He was the main breadwinner in our family, and despite my own desire to succeed, I knew at this point his career had to come first. Nursery drop-offs and pick-ups were my responsibility, as was running our house, managing our finances and doing my day job. It wasn't easy, but I just soldiered through in the hope that the rough times would pass.

After six months of working in London, I took my daughter

out of her nursery. One of the carers at the nursery was fed up with her job and wanted to become a full-time childminder. I seized the opportunity to convince her to come and work for me. Although it wasn't confirmed at the time, I suspected I was pregnant with our second child. There was no way I could afford the £1,300 per month that two places in nursery would cost me, never mind the cost of travel into London. I knew I could afford to pay her to look after both my children four days a week and she would make more than she was earning at the nursery, plus it would alleviate some of the pressure on me to get home at a certain time.

By the time my second pregnancy was confirmed, I had been working for Roy for just over a year. The programme office was now set up, and we were up and running in terms of project deliveries. It was only a matter of time before most of our projects would complete and the rest of the work would slowly be transitioned back into business as usual, so it seemed unlikely that there would be a role for me to come back to. Roy assured me he would use his contacts to help me find a suitable role within the firm when I was ready to return. I was now fully proficient in running and setting up PMOs, and my next step would be to become a PMO manager. My performance reviews had placed me in the top quartile of talent in an organisation with over 10,000 employees. When I went on maternity leave the second time, it was on a career high. There was no way I was going to return to another basement shuffling papers this time, I made that abundantly clear before I left and during my maternity leave.

Pregnancy was harder the second time around. I had eventually lost all the baby weight from my first pregnancy, only to put on 110 pounds during my second pregnancy. By the time I got to the seven months' pregnant mark, it was the height of the hottest summer the UK had seen for 30 years and I was nothing short of huge. The 10-minute walk to work and back was probably the hardest part of my day because I couldn't walk at a normal speed. I would press the button at the pedestrian crossing to cross the road, the beeps would start and before I was even halfway across the road, the oncoming traffic would start again.

I was tested for every medical ailment known to man as they couldn't quite understand why I was putting on such an extraordinary amount of weight. I had my own suspicions – I ate for the 16 hours I was awake each day. Being pregnant meant I didn't have to watch my weight and it was great not to worry what I was eating for the second time in my life however, I knew the price I would pay once the baby was born and the weight would have to come off.

After numerous tests the doctors concluded that baby number two was about 11lb. at 37 weeks and had to come out. They convinced me to have a caesarean as opposed to the natural birth I had with Mia as they were worried whether I could deliver a baby of such a size. I had to disagree, safe in the knowledge that my hips and backside had their own postcode. My second daughter was born a week early, a decent 8lb. 1oz., hardly the mammoth they predicted. I was furious as I was aware that the C section would have been more painful post-birth than having a baby naturally, plus I wouldn't have been able to drive or get back into my routine quickly. I also already had a two-year-old, so being incapacitated was never going to be an option.

There were no issues with my maternal instinct the second time around. I was much more confident. Part of me was very content as I fully intended to enjoy this maternity leave with both my children. Returning to work was on my agenda in the coming months, but now I had a lot more options on directions my career could now take. I had three sets of skills I could exploit, and I was part of an organisation that was full of opportunities. I also now had numerous champions such as my two previous bosses whom I trusted to help me when the time came.

I stayed off work with my second child for four months which, in hindsight, was too short. Having my second child was slightly easier in the respect that I had my childminder with me from day one to help. Having an extra set of hands also enabled me to start to lose the baby weight. Losing the weight was actually harder than managing both kids. As a UK size 22, I would take both children out in the double buggy, running up hills and walking the three miles back and forth into the town whenever I had an errand to run. They loved it, whereas most of the time I was blue and couldn't breathe! As some of the weight came off, my walking turned to jogging (or shuffling as I called it). I also re-joined Weight Watchers. Their diet was a formula I was comfortable with as I had used it to help lose the weight from my first pregnancy. It fitted in with my lifestyle and eating preferences, so that part was easy. It was transitioning from shuffling to actually jogging - that was the tough bit. I knew I needed something which would exercise all of me, and I knew it had to be something I could combine with other things I had to do, like going to the shops. Still weighing a whopping 220 pounds, I was no Paula Radcliffe. I looked more like I had eaten an entire running team. The first time I went out to jog I got one mile up the road and had to take the bus back. Stewart opened the door and I was in tears, telling him that I didn't think I could lose the weight this time.

Slowly but surely it did come off, one to two pounds a week. One mile turned into two miles, two miles turned into three, and before I knew it my jogging had turned into running. The fitter I got, the more energy I found I had. Once I had managed to run without stopping for 20 minutes, I booked myself on a series of charity five-kilometre and ten-kilometre runs through my local running club. Having those runs in the diary gave me the incentive I needed to stick with it as I didn't want to let anyone down, let alone those who had sponsored me. Although I was still overweight, just before I returned to work I ran my first ever half marathon in two hours and 30 minutes. This was quite an achievement given the fact I couldn't run to the ice cream van less than four months earlier.

I stayed in touch with Roy and Elaine and all the other contacts I had made throughout my maternity leave, once again making it clear that I wanted to return and that I wanted a juicy opportunity. I would even consider working full time, but I needed at least one of those days working from home.

The call came from my boss about three weeks before I was due to return. He told me that while I'd been off my company had won the bid to transition the IT services of European Bank. They had had the account for approximately three months but it wasn't going well. Cultural issues had surfaced that I'd seen first hand before when they took over my old company and nothing was moving fast. Two of the previous PMO directors had left the programme, and they needed someone to go in and sort out the portfolio alongside a hotshot programme director they were flying in from the US. They needed someone who knew the ropes, someone who could hit the ground running, and moreover deal with the key stakeholders who were not engaging with their new colleagues.

I was already checking train times and trying my still too tight suit before the phone went down. I wanted this job. That said, I wasn't going to forgo the needs of my children, I fully planned to negotiate my corner in terms of my return. My terms were four days a week plus one from home, and if I had responsibilities with the children, those took priority. They agreed, and between us we set a date for my return.

I was so excited. This was the job, the job I had wanted for 12 years. I was heading back into London, working in the City, as a PMO manager in IT at a bank. Yes, all the fears were still there and the weight wasn't entirely off yet, but I put all of that to the back of my mind. I was now in a position to pick up the reins of my career and go for it. My family was complete, I had secure childcare, Stewart was doing well in his job and finally I had reached a point when I could now climb up the career ladder, and I intended to do it at lightning speed.

SUCCESS, BUT AT WHAT COST?

My integration back into work the second time was relatively smooth. Everything I thought I had forgotten slowly began to return. I loved being back in the City, I loved putting on my suit every morning, and above all I loved the prospect of getting my career back on track now that my family was complete. I still missed the kids terribly, but I saw work as a necessary evil if I ever wanted to give them the things I never had as a child. I saw each day as an opportunity to grow and learn and grab every opportunity that came my way.

I met my new boss, Jake, on the third day of my first week. His reputation preceded him. I'd been told he was a smartly dressed, charming individual who was delivery orientated and not someone who suffered fools gladly. The man I met was all of that and more! He was a focused and driven Chicago native who was clearly very experienced and had, in his words, come to this account in the UK 'to sort this shit out'.

When he spoke, he spoke with incredible drive and enthusiasm. I couldn't help but be in awe of him. This was the kind of leader I wanted to work for. He was someone who was going places and I wanted him to take me with him. Despite my fondness for my previous bosses who all had their own good qualities, Jake was different. He had a fire in his belly and a passion to succeed like no one I had ever met. I recognised myself in him. Together, I wanted us to be the A-Team – no matter how big the mountain was, we would get to the top and probably dance on our way up. If you have ever met someone who could be talking about the most boring subjects and yet still have the ability to captivate you and make you feel like you are part of the most exciting journey in the world, that was Jake. He could sell snow to Eskimos and then buy it back at a discount! I, for one, was sold.

I couldn't wait to work for him, to learn from him and to see his plans for how we were going to sort out this pear-shaped programme and make it a success in just a few months. All eyes were on us. The pressure to turn the programme around and deliver was coming from on high, and we didn't dare fail. You could almost smell the fear and excitement as we worked through our plan of action, participating in hours and hours of workshops where Jake encouraged us all to brainstorm. Jake knew that if he could motivate the team, include their ideas and show them what an integral part of the journey they all were, then he would ultimately succeed.

I watched as he built his relationships with the bank's stakeholders, ignoring the 'them and us' culture that always exists when a third party or outsourcer arrives. He listened to their previous frustrations and made commitments to put things right. He was a man of his word and whatever it took to right the wrongs, he took responsibility to ensure it was done. It was then that I learned the value of delivering quick wins in a project in order to get teams and key stakeholders on board. I also learned the value of publicising successes. If you start by admitting that something needs improvement, then any achievement, no matter how small, is a step in the right direction and worth shouting about!

During the first few weeks Jake gave me challenges that were well beyond my abilities and tasks that stretched me in ways I never anticipated. Some of those challenges involved additional study in the evenings. He encouraged me to learn so I fully understood the technical aspects that would enable me to challenge others and ultimately make me more successful in my role. From a leadership perspective, he gave me responsibility, he made me accountable for my actions and above all, he trusted me as he knew that if I hit a brick wall I would come back and ask for his help.

Over the next few months as we battled to build relationships and get mobilised, I was forever at his side. I watched his every move, shadowed him in meetings and observed how he approached things, especially sticky staff situations. This was the more interesting part. Jake was very passionate about his craft, and often with passionate people when things don't go their way it can spill over and manifest itself as other emotions. Jake was known for having a temper. His temper could flare from nothing if he felt people were not as committed to the programme goals as he was. It got to a point where any bad news was delivered through me, as I was the only one close enough to him to rationalise his response.

The programme itself involved removing a number of computer servers from a multitude of locations, including under people's desks, and housing them in the outsourcing company's data centres. Doing this was going to save the outsourcing company a significant amount of money as there would be fewer servers to maintain and any issues were easier to administer and control from an IT perspective. Our job was to take 800 servers out of the bank's IT hardware estate over a period of four months. Some of the servers would be decommissioned (i.e. switched off entirely and no longer used), others would just be moved as they were, or their applications would be migrated on to other servers. Since it wasn't just a case of switching them off, each server had to be analysed, planned for and then moved. This process was managed by a team of highly qualified project managers and various teams of technical staff.

Our biggest problem was that the programme hadn't been resourced adequately for the technical work to be done within the set time-frame. We appeared to have an overflow of project managers, but no actual technical doers. In addition to working within the PMO and with the project managers, my role was to scour the City to find good technical people who were available almost immediately. It was more than a challenge, as good people aren't generally sitting at home waiting for their next role. It normally takes a few months to find the right people, wait for their notice periods to end, and get them on board and up to speed, however we didn't have that kind of time.

I engaged with virtually every recruitment company across the City, and spent days and days filtering CVs and conducting what can only be described as dull technical interviews in order to secure and hire the people we needed to deliver the programme. Over the next six weeks the team started to fall into place. A sea of Unix administrators, Windows engineers and programmers began to arrive and get stuck into our migration plan. By month two, I had grown the technical team from three to 20. Even looking back now, I am not sure how I pulled off that amount of hiring in such a short period of time.

Now that we had the people on site, our next task was to start our programme in earnest. Each month we had a target number of servers to be removed across London and Europe that counted towards the overall total. When those targets weren't met, Jake's temper would turn into a fireball. I had to tell him four days before the month end that we were not going make our target. We had experienced problems in our European office and we were going to be short by about 10 servers. His face went bright red as he banged his hands on his laptop before hurtling a stapler across the room. He didn't scare me with his outbursts; by this point I had dealt with far worse situations and I knew this was just frustration on his part and had nothing to do with me personally. He was dedicated to making this programme a success, and the quicker he did it, the quicker he could go back to Chicago with a feather in his cap.

I worked on the account for five months, and as we headed towards the final goals for the programme it was time for Jake to go on to another account back in the US. Part of me wanted to go with him. Under his tutelage I found out what I was capable of, renewed my passion for IT, learned how to work under extreme pressure and finally got my confidence back after returning from maternity leave.

His departure had a big impact on my morale. I missed the excitement of the daily firefights we faced and his hilarious temper tantrums too. Discussions were starting on the next big programme, and although I was still part of the original team, I knew I was starting to hanker after the next big thing.

A new programme manager arrived, and as with most people who take on a new leadership role, he took his broom out and started to sweep clean, unpicking teams and breaking down processes that had taken months to establish and embed in order to run a model that he was more familiar with. It felt like watching someone demolish the house you had built brick by brick. The pressure was off by this point as the account was relatively on track, the team was well established and most of the hard work was done. Even though I respected the new programme manager's experience, I knew I wouldn't have the same kind of relationship with him as I'd had with Jake. I also knew that if I wanted my career to progress it was time to move on from the company.

I wanted to work directly for a bank and not work at a bank as part of a third party organisation. Outsource staff were not allowed to transfer across to their internal customers in this company, so I knew I would have to make an external move. Things were still in order at home, and after discussions with Stewart, he agreed to stay in his existing role to enable me to make the next big jump in my career. His actual words were: "Now it's your turn." I knew this also meant I was going back to work full time because there was no way any bank at that time would consider a part-time role. This meant more compromise at home in terms of increasing our childcare, but it was a decision we took as a family.

Having worked with a number of recruiters during my time at the bank, I had much better relationships in place to help me find another role. It took me exactly four weeks from deciding to move to being offered a role as a PMO in IT at a leading US investment bank.

When I resigned, I was summoned to a lunch with the new programme manager who, I had heard, was going to attempt to convince me to stay. After he had spent an hour presenting a feeble business case about what the future held for the programme, he then changed his tune and basically told me that the main reason I shouldn't leave was that he didn't believe I would ever make it in the cut-throat world of investment banking. His sales pitch continued with him telling me that I would be much better off staying with him as he had a number of administrative tasks that needed doing! I sat back in my chair and had to hold up my chin to stop my jaw from dropping. Experience had taught me to thank him for his opinion but say that my decision was final. I was going to take my chances and if it all fell through, then I would just do as I have always done, pick myself up and try and try again. If anything, his comments just spurred me on to make it work.

I swore to myself from that moment on that for every person who told me what I couldn't do, I would set myself an amazing goal, either personally or professionally, and I would achieve it. Over time, I ended up with a lot of challenges! I decided that rather than take any notice of the doubters, that I would use their opinions to fuel my passions and desire to succeed, and in the long term prove them wrong!

My new boss, a business manager for IT at my new bank, was yet another unique individual. He was an ex-public school boy with ambition and huge aspirations, and he was also desperate to prove that he could take on a role bigger than the one he was currently in. I was only five months into the role when he was finally offered a big job and a move to the US. I had been doing a great job in the PMO and assisting him in business management, helping to get a $48m portfolio of change under control and implement the much-needed structure and processes that are required for a portfolio of that size. I had assumed that, as I was doing so well, it would be logical for me to transition directly into his role. I had all the skills, all the experience plus I had started to build and embed relationships with the leadership team and others across the firm.

For whatever reason, he made the decision to go out to the job market to backfill his role. I was extremely disappointed that he didn't take a chance on me. I suggested that he let me try and run with the role for a couple of months alongside my other responsibilities, but he just didn't bite. Instead he opted to bring in an external chap who was paid £20k more than I was earning for doing more or less the same job.

The individual only lasted three months and when they got rid of him, you can guess who was left to pick up the pieces, executing exactly what I had suggested less than three months before. This was the first time I witnessed the art of paying people off if they turned out to be bad hires, or if the line manager didn't want to go through the arduous task that is managing poor performance. The real world of bank life and the oddities within it continued to unfold!

I loved my new role and now that I had global responsibilities, I found myself having to travel to the US. It was the first time I had left the children, now four and two, and I struggled with the prospect of being away from them all week. I had travelled to Europe in my previous roles but only ever for one or two days since the birth of the children. This trip would be a whole seven days without them. We discussed it as a family, and Stewart told me had no issues with coping with the kids and working. He acknowledged that this was an important time for my career and that I needed to go and build relationships with my peer group overseas. I prepared as much as I could and promised to phone every day.

Walking through Heathrow in my suit heading off to the Business Class lounge was a totally new experience. I had a suitcase of papers, a suitcase of suits and a bag of guilt that I would not be able to check in. In spite of my excitement there was a still a part of me that was questioning my role as a mother versus my career. What if I would be expected to travel to the US frequently, how would I balance the travel with family life?

I will never forget getting on the plane and turning left to my little pod in Business Class. There's something about hearing those hallowed words, "Would you like a glass of champagne, madam?" from the flight attendant for the very first time that lets you know you've reached another corporate milestone. I think I played with all the buttons in my seat for the first hour of the flight. The other passengers must have thought I was nuts. The guy opposite me offered to help me after watching the screen that separated our seats go up and down five or six times. "First time?" he asked. "Erm, yes," I mumbled, rather embarrassed that I looked like a kid in a sweet shop. It turned out he also knew my new boss back at the office, so that made it even more cringe-worthy!

On the way back from the US after a series of meetings and dinners I was starting to realise that I was in quite an important role. If I focused and worked hard, this could actually be the company where I could work my way up to vice president, director and maybe even higher. With this in mind, I thought about when I first met Jake and the impression he'd made on me (and everyone else) with his well-cut suit, his immaculate shoes and briefcase and, most memorably for me, his pen. It was a Mont Blanc. It occurred to me that I had seen a number of senior individuals with these pens, and I figured that if I was going to start to build my brand as a future executive I would need all the trimmings. I bought myself my first Mont Blanc pen on that flight and I still have it today, 11 years later. I remember trying to rationalise my extravagant purchase to Stewart when I got home. His only words were "How much??" Little did he know that it wouldn't be the last time he would ask that question as my quest to fit into the corporate world and build my own brand continued.

After picking up the pieces for a couple of months and running with the role, there was more change to come. Something was brewing. Suddenly there were projects with code names and the leadership team was being ushered into secret meetings here, there and everywhere. Whatever was coming our way was clearly going to be big.

Within weeks they announced that our part of the bank was going to be acquired by another US bank. This US bank had no previous UK presence, it was strong in fixed income but not in equities where our strengths were, and it had no real global presence either, which made our little operation a perfect fit. Their reputation was elitist to say the least. They were known for only ever hiring from Harvard or Yale, their people were the best of the best and their growth story to date had been nothing short of amazing. They were coming to the UK to put their stamp on the world of UK finance, and the competition was well within its rights to be scared. With their state-of-the-art IT, money-management systems and no-nonsense approach, little did we know our acquisition would be just the start of their amazing journey, one that would take them to the top of their field in less than four years.

When the announcement came, everyone went into panic mode. It was the normal fears that almost brought all work to a standstill. The key topic of conversation by every watercooler was how the new people would sack us all and put their people in our jobs, how differently they would do things and that nothing would ever be the same. Some individuals voted with their feet and left, others hung around to see what it would be like, and others stayed put to hold out for potential redundancy. Very few were jumping for joy.

I have never been one to get out my 'the end of the world is nigh' sandwich board when faced with a challenge, nor did I want to join in with a misery fest before I knew the facts of the situation. I wanted to make up my own mind about whether the takeover was a good thing or a bad thing. My default position was positivity first until proven otherwise, and if it turned out to be a bad thing then I would just move on. I believe I was one of only a few people that quickly became excited about the prospect of this new name coming to take over our part of the bank. Having been in a similar situation before, I knew the amount of opportunities that this could present. It would mean new people, a new culture and new things to learn.

As the deal was confirmed and new faces started to arrive, I welcomed them with open arms. I did everything I could to help them understand our people, existing processes, projects and structures, as well as sharing the challenges we currently faced.

I quickly became acquainted with the new team and senior management and as a consequence, I had identified myself as a go-to person for navigating the division. I caught a lot of flak from my original colleagues at the time. The perception was that I was ensuring that my backside was covered so I could secure a key role in the future organisation. To me, I was just doing my job. These were my new employers, they were taking over whether we liked it or not, so I thought it was within all our interests to help them to settle in. That would allow us to get back to supporting the business and normality as soon as possible.

The process of merging the two banks was set to be done over an ambitious three months. All of their staff were US based and were staying there – no one was migrated. The bulk of the work needed was around decoupling our IT systems from our previous bank and re-attaching ourselves to theirs. Sounds easy, but not when you think that the IT infrastructure had taken years to build, and now we had less than three months to do what some people anticipated should take a year. The timeline set the tone of the incoming organisation: they knew what they wanted and they wanted it done quickly. It was a real wake-up call to what had been a sleepy department that previously just ticked over.

By that point I had joined the leadership team in a supporting role. My job was to make the seven directors effective by removing the tedious tasks that held them back from doing their jobs. It was a 'whatever it takes' kind of role with no two days being the same. I have always loved variety in my roles, so this position played to all of my strengths.

It was wonderful opportunity and a great place to observe from if you were an individual still learning the ropes. I got to help shape decisions without having direct responsibility for their execution.

I have always been a people watcher, and this merger was prime viewing. Watching the various individuals within my team jostle for positions and opportunities to impress our new company was like car crash TV at times. Previously there had been very little competition and to be fair, they had all worked together quite contently as the kings and queens of their own little chiefdoms. Now not only were they going to be forced to work together, there was also another set of individuals who knew just as much as they did, with their own relationships already embedded, coming in to integrate with the existing team.

The new firm chose one of the existing team members to take over the leadership team when our existing chief technology officer (CTO) opted to move back to the mothership of our old firm.

The new CTO had his work cut out given the expectations of the new firm. The initial challenge he faced was managing his new team, as prior to his appointment, they were his peer group. Almost every head of function he now had to manage was a highly skilled corporate politician. Each of them had their own personal agenda that didn't include their ex-colleague being at the helm. Watching the dynamics and behaviours of these people was truly fascinating. I wasn't sure whether I should be shocked by what I was witnessing or grateful for the opportunity to see how the game was really played. I would observe them when I sat in meetings like a female David Attenborough, watching them metaphorically displaying their peacock feathers as they jostled for power and position. I started to wonder if this was what I should be learning if I was ever going to make it on to an executive team. Perhaps this was the other side of corporate life that no one taught you: you had to be in it to win it. It was becoming increasingly obvious that the ones who played the game well enough survived and the ones who chose not to play left the organisation with a nicely worded corporate obituary.

Despite attempts by a couple of the CTO's team to make his life difficult, he found his feet and began to pull his management team together. I knew him fairly well and we got on OK, however we certainly weren't buddies – my former role within the PMO had involved policing his projects and programmes, therefore we had gone head-to-head a couple of times in the past.

I still viewed his promotion as an opportunity. He had limited supporters lower down in the organisation, therefore if he was going to pull off this amazing IT integration he was going to need all the support he could get, and above all, a route to the people. Who better than me to help him get it done?

I tried to tempt him with ideas of things we could do and smaller projects that I could run as we moved into what can only be described as three months of blood, sweat and tears. He wasn't even remotely interested. Eventually I asked for a meeting with him one-to-one to find out why he wasn't giving me the opportunities I thought I deserved. He responded with his usual frown alongside a few painful moments of silence – the kind of silence during which you wonder if you have just said something that marks the beginning of the end of your career.

He looked up at me and said: "OK. If you want a chance to prove to me what you are really made of, take over business continuity while we work out how we will manage it once we are integrated with the new firm." I knew business continuity was about keeping everything running in the event of an incident, but that was about as far as it went. I thought it was worth flagging up that I didn't know anything about business continuity, to which he replied: "If you have a point to prove, you will learn."

I took on business continuity. I bought books and reached out to my limited IT network to find out what the role entailed. All I knew was that a series of tests needed to be run where we would take all of our IT systems down and then bring them back up again – the theory being that everything should work effectively after that process. I would also have to run a workplace recovery test, which meant relocating key staff to an alternative building and ensuring that in the event of a crisis we could still run our business. The final part was ensuring all of the business units had plans so they knew how to respond in the case of an emergency and who the individuals were within their departments who would keep the business afloat until we got back on our feet. Within three months all tests were run, new processes were implemented and it wasn't long before I found myself back in his office, smugly asking him if I had passed the test and what my next challenge would be. He said: "Your biggest test is yet to come. Now get back to your day job, as we all have to ensure the integration goes as smoothly as possible. Oh, and by the way, well done." At last, a bit of recognition from the man of steel.

From a personal perspective, I was spending a huge amount of time with the leadership team and technical teams as we sped towards the integration deadline. I would work 14 hours a day and often return home long after the kids had gone to bed. I didn't see them in the morning and I didn't see them in the evening and most of my weekends were spent at work. I was tired and my mind was elsewhere and I had lost the will and ability to communicate with Stewart when I was at home. All I was focused on was what I had to do the next day and being back in the office at 7am. I knew that if I did well over the next couple of months there was a fair chance I would get promoted in December, and I wanted that promotion to show the fruits of my labour more than anything.

I remember testing with Hong Kong at 4am, only surviving on copious cans of Red Bull to keep me awake. During this time I was so into my career and my own progress that I had totally disappeared up my own backside – even I didn't know who I was anymore. All I knew was that I was now part of the leadership team; I thought like them, I acted like them, I wore a suit that made me look like a bloke and half of the decisions I made were shaped by others as opposed to what I actually felt was right. My spare time after work involved winding down over too many glasses of wine with my colleagues who had basically become my new family. Problems I would normally have discussed at home were discussed with them; time I should have spent at home was spent with them. I literally lived and breathed my work and my team. I had lost my way, and myself, and at the time I just couldn't see it.

Commitments for the children's activities such as sports days were disguised in my diary as doctor's appointments. There were countless occasions when the kids were ill and Stewart and I would argue about whose day and meetings were more important, and whoever lost got to stay at home and look after the children – it should not have even been a conversation. It was always about that oh-so-important meeting that just couldn't be missed for fear of being left out of a decision being made; it all contributed to what had become a set of really screwed-up priorities.

I was very much alone with most of my decisions, and the only people close enough that I could have talked to were generally part of the problem. There were no women at all at my level at the time, and certainly no working mums, so I didn't have any role models or anyone to confide in. I was just finding my way and trying to avoid making mistakes, picking up tips about how things were done from the boys who didn't face the same challenges or responsibilities as I did. I really could have used some guidance, someone to steer me in the right direction and keep me in check.

The integration date drew close. All of us were tired from our extensive work schedules and the fact we hadn't seen much of our home lives for months. One afternoon I was sitting at my desk after having yet another argument with Stewart about not coming home and I looked at myself, sitting there with my flash pen, Mont Blanc filofax and handmade pinstriped waistcoated suit thinking what on earth have I become? I was just a step away from everything I thought I ever wanted, but I was starting to recognise that it had cost me something.

Relations between Stewart and me were in tatters. He had supported me in my career, often taking a back seat to enable me to progress, and was this how I repaid him? Leaving him behind while I was absorbed in my own career, eaten up by my own desire for the next job title and competing with the egos of those around me. I stood at the foot of London Bridge at 3am after another night of rigorous testing, in tears as I felt that I had dug myself a hole that I couldn't get out of. I felt I had a choice to make. I either needed to repair my family and get back to the real me, or face a lonely existence with only my embossed business card to keep me company.

The integration came and went. It wasn't without emergencies which involved even longer hours to remediate, but by and large the team had pulled it off to much rapturous self applause and back-patting. The teams and staff were now left to pick up the pieces of their shattered home lives and sleep for days in the hope that all their efforts would result in promotions and decent numbers at bonus time. I kept telling Stewart that the whole reason I worked so hard was to get my promotion and a decent bonus. I assured him that our rocky patch had not been for nothing and all my hard work would be rewarded.

Promotion time came, and I remember my boss sitting opposite me telling me that I didn't get the promotion: "Vanessa," he said, "it's just not your turn this year. Work harder and next year it will come." "Work harder? Work harder?" I asked in total disbelief. "I have given the company the very essence of my soul and every ounce of energy I had for the last five months." I felt like someone had harpooned me in the heart. Fighting back the tears, I left the room to make my way home to Stewart. I sat on the train preparing for how I would tell him that after everything I had done and everything we had been through, I hadn't even been promoted. It was all for nothing. I felt so stupid and let down. It was a situation that seemed like the end of the world at the time.

In spite of the fact that I hadn't seen friends or family for months, and half of them didn't even like the person I had become (including my mum), they rallied to support me. Stewart told me that we could get through it together, but we needed to take stock and work out what our next steps would be. He made it abundantly clear that I had to change. I had to rein in my ambition and my deep need to prove all my doubters wrong. Personally, I didn't even know what success looked like anymore because whenever I achieved anything I just wanted more. I was caught up in this horrid cycle of wishing, wanting, getting, and wishing again! It suddenly felt like a shallow existence.

I felt broken. Everything I had ever worked for and wanted felt like it had been drained out of me. Things had to change, and I knew that the only person who could make that change was me – but change to what exactly?

RESILIENCE

I stayed at my company for another year. I cut back my ridiculous hours and reduced my deep-rooted desire to take on everything after reflecting on the previous year's *annus horribilis*. I needed time to reflect, lick my wounds and rethink my career strategy. I was still intent on getting my promotion, but I wasn't going to fall for presenteeism or a take on a ball-breaking demeanour to achieve it. And I certainly wasn't going to risk losing my family.

Although he hadn't promoted me, it was clear the CTO had full faith in me to deliver. I had become his right-hand woman and I had a multitude of valuable skills that could be used across his organisation. I had also made it abundantly clear that if I didn't get my promotion the next time around, I would walk. I had embedded myself so much into the fabric of the division that I knew the prospect of me leaving would feel like he was losing his right arm, just when he needed it most.

As before, he continued to drop me into projects and to run departments where I had little or no experience. It was a great opportunity. He likened it to being 'helicoptered in' – going in like the SAS, performing a rescue mission and getting out. My role was exactly that. I would arrive on the scene, find out what was going on and what needed to be improved, I would then report back to him and make my recommendations. The bit he failed to mention at the outset was that, more often than not, I would also be the one to execute what I had recommended as well as running the department until a full-time replacement could be sourced.

I was helicoptered into the IT service delivery department, which consisted of around 15 staff spread across three sub-functions. Two of the staff resigned within the first week of me arriving. I stayed with the department as we looked at core processes and created a plan to clear a three-month backlog of requests. Just as Jake would have done back in those days, we identified quick wins and shared our plans in a bid to change the perception of this department by our own internal department and wider business. Together we rebuilt the department from the ground up, chipping away at the backlog piece by piece, alongside campaigning for the resources we needed so the existing team could stop working weekends. Eventually we got there, with reputation and service restored, all in time for one of the leadership team to come and officially take over the department and, of course, take complete credit for its new well-oiled state!

I wasn't particularly popular in my helicopter role. People often thought I was a spy for the CTO, seeking out poor performers and then subsequently getting rid of them. I was rarely welcomed with open arms, and some people would initially do their best to sabotage my efforts and stop me finding their departmental and people issues. This often changed when they realised I was actually on their side and my job was just to help them wade through the treacle and start delivering. It was a thankless task and the only one who applauded the results was the CTO. Having me fix his departments one by one freed him up to focus on other things, like building relationships with our new employers and running his own wayward team.

On a personal level, despite the variety in my role and the fact I did eventually get promoted that year, I still wasn't happy. My gut feeling was telling me I needed to get out of what I now deemed to be a toxic environment. Emotionally there was too much of me wrapped up in my job and in the firm itself. I also knew by the way I looked and acted that I had spent far too long in the company of high-flying men. I felt like I had more or less become one, swapping all of those amazing feminine traits I once had for a more egotistical and manipulative way of working. It didn't feel like the real me, I knew that much.

Despite its ups and downs, working in finance and banking did have its perks and good times. I had learned so much over the past 20 years and had the opportunity to interact with so many amazing people, some of whom I still consider my dearest friends and mentors today. From a financial perspective it was great. We had been able to move to a slightly bigger house, we drove cars that didn't break down all of the time and we had nicer holidays. My mum and the kids didn't want for anything, and my handbag and shoe collection were becoming something most women would die for. However, despite my belief as a child, having money doesn't cure everything and nor does it make you particularly happy. Despite the income, I wasn't doing a job I was passionate about and nor did I have the kind of people around me that would bring out the best in me.

I was also starting to realise how much I missed my interactions with women. I often wondered if things would have been any different if I had had another woman in the leadership team or a role model I could have confided in. Would I still have ended up as the emotionless clone and career nut? There had been a woman on the original leadership team whom I really admired, a lovely lady who was very supportive to me during her tenure. But like so many other senior women I met over the years, she became bored of the politics and threw her cards in just before the merger, choosing to set up her own business and be her own boss. I think she saw what was coming long before I did.

Outside of my day job, I had been thinking for a while about the possibility of a business venture of my own, something that Stewart and I could potentially set up together that would unite us with a joint interest. I pictured a business that we could build alongside our corporate careers that would eventually be an earner in its own right, and over time perhaps even enable one or both of us to leave the rat-race for good. I had no idea at the time what this might be, nor was I aware of any gaps in the market that we could potentially exploit.

After returning from a weekend of brainstorming potential business ideas, I decided to look at the job market as an alternative to setting up my own business. Whatever I did next, I knew it involved leaving my current role. I sought the advice of a friend called Maggie Berry who ran the IT women's network and job board, Women In Technology. The main purpose of the meeting was initially to see what was in the market so I could change roles. During our conversation, I was telling her about my frustrations and the fact that despite wanting to continue in the corporate world, I was harbouring another niggle whereby I felt this deep need to do something in the world that actually counted. I also explained how day after day I would look out of my window across to my other building where 'the business' resided and think how do I get from my back office IT world over there to the front office? How do I learn what they do in fixed income or equities when my bosses don't believe it's relevant to my current role? With no training budget allocated to aspiration, how do I learn new things other than my normal method of buying books and studying in the evenings? Even if I did all of that, how would it solve this other desire to do something for the good of the world?

She advised me to try looking at a couple of the women's networks that existed across the City, as these provided opportunities to meet new people and learn new skills. I remember snarling at the thought. "Women's networks?" I asked. "Don't they burn bras and effigies of men? Why would I want to waste my time with those?" She laughed and told me not to knock something before I had tried it. I went back to the office, still thinking about women's networks, but I couldn't get the vision of a coven-like group out of my head, baking cakes in the back of a church or knitting in unison.

I checked Google for women's networks as a starting point and a raft of information came up on my screen. There were so many different groups I could join: networks that were industry-centric or role-specific; networks that were aimed at minority groups; networks, think tanks, networks and more networks! It was information overload.

I wondered where all these female groups had been hiding, and why wasn't I aware of them before? If they were as good as everyone seemed to be saying they were on the internet, what a missed opportunity on my part! Then I realised why I wasn't aware of them: it might have had something to do with having my head up my own backside for the past three years, and my only network being predominantly male and inside my own building. What also surprised me about the information I was reading online was the amount of women that were forming these groups in a bid to help out other women. It felt like I had discovered the start of a small but apparently effective revolution.

As I waded through the pages and pages of options, I started to wonder what would happen if I chose to invest time away from the children and Stewart to attend some of these events. How could I be sure that I would get a return on my time investment? How would I meet the right peer group? Would these women welcome me, considering that I was an alpha female desperate to find her inner woman? It was hugely frustrating going through each site trying to find the right network for me. The closest I got to something that looked like the right fit was Women in Banking and Finance, so I joined. It did cross my mind at this point how useful it would have been if there was a website that centralised all this information for the benefit of time-strapped women like me so I wouldn't have had to waste so much of my time researching.

Stewart and I had booked our annual weekend away without the kids. We had made a promise that even if it was only once a year, we would endeavour to get away on our own to just be Vanessa and Stewart. No one's son and daughter, no one's mum and dad, no one's employee – just us. This time we were off to a lovely boutique hotel in the north of Spain for our much-needed time together.

While we were in Spain, and over a fair few bottles of wine, I was still rattling on about the fact I felt this need to do something else. I was moaning that despite the wonder of the internet, I'd had trouble sourcing the information I needed in order to pinpoint a networking group to attend that would really be worth my while. I had by that point given in to that fact that I was going to try the women's networks as a starting point to find that elusive 'something else'.

After an hour of listening to me witter on, Stewart told me to stop whingeing and suggested I just accept the fact that some of these networks could be a waste of time for me; however, some could be just what I was looking for. He then added: "While you are on your voyage of discovery around the networks, why don't you document what you find for the benefit of other women, and we will put it on a website? There must be thousands of women who are feeling exactly like you, so you would be doing them all a favour." More wine followed, and before we knew it, the idea of documenting my journey had snowballed. It wasn't just about me capturing details of all the women's networks and their events; it would be about collating all sorts of information that would benefit City women. We could build a website for time-poor women that focused on both their career needs and personal needs. By the time the sun went down we had mapped out on two pieces of A5 paper what we would include if we built a website purely for women.

I was so excited. I rang a few City girls and PAs I knew to bounce the idea of our website off them. Calling 40 friends from Spain is a very expensive way to do your market research, or so I found out when I got my £800 phone bill a month later. After a few hours of phone calls, we knew we had indeed found a gap in the market.

Sobriety dawned the following day and the initial buzz of our idea wore off as we packed our bags and headed back to the UK. Why is it you always feel like you can solve all of the world's problems or come up with the next ground-breaking idea after a few glasses of wine?

Monday morning came, back at my desk, and once again I was dreaming of the day before when Stewart and I were basking in the Spanish sun. I started to think about our business idea. Would it work? Was it needed? Or was it just me that felt the need to have all of the information I was trying to find in one place? Just as I was deep in thought, an email arrived from Stewart.

From: Stewart Vallely
To: Vanessa Vallely
Date: 12 March 2008

Re: I bought you a couple of presents

Excited, I read on, expecting another night away or something similar. I continued to read.

I bought you www.womeninthecity.co.uk and www.wearethecity.com

Pick which one you like and let's do something about it. An idea is just an idea until you do something about it!

Love

Stewart xx

I looked at the email and thought, well, it's not flowers, it's not a weekend away in another hot country, but he is in IT, so I suppose I shouldn't expect much else in terms of presents than website domains. However, it did make me realise that he was serious about our idea and he was encouraging me to drive it forward.

The fact we now owned two website domains was indeed the first real step of the journey. We could have just filed them with the two pieces of A5 paper and put it down to a batty idea that we never did anything else about. I investigated both names and found there was already a well-established women's annual luncheon club running under the name of Women In The City, so the idea to use that as our brand had to be shelved. I liked WeAreTheCity as it felt like quite a strong statement, and one which I wanted to shout from the rooftops: "Actually, it's not just about men here, it's as much about women. We are the City too!!"

The name stuck, and over the course of the next week, Stewart began to build our website on a low-cost website builder called Moonfruit. At first it was very blue and grey, and when I first saw the prototype it said one thing to me: Masculine.

Together Stewart and I worked to pink it up a little, changing the hard lines to soft boxes, taking out the black and replacing it with a softer grey. In terms of content, I started to scour all of those internet sites I had visited less than three weeks before looking for potential content. I wrote to over 100 women's networks asking them if they wanted to be featured on our new website for women. Only a few of them replied. The frostiest responses I received were from a few networks who dictated a certain level of education or a certain job title in order to join. I kept thinking that surely these networks needed to be more inclusive, especially in terms of encouraging and nurturing the future pipeline of women. How could the next generation of women even get started if they didn't have access to the experiences of these senior women?! I vowed at that point that WeAreTheCity would be open to everyone. Be it a shelf-stacker in a supermarket or a counter girl with aspirations, we would welcome them equally alongside our corporate workers. Women are women and they all have desires and dreams, regardless of where their careers start.

Not everyone understood our amazing idea. I remember

a phone call to my best friend about what would eventually be WeAreTheCity. My excitement was spilling over down the phone as I explained the concept to her and told her what we had built so far. Imagine a balloon filled to bursting with air, and someone comes along and sticks a big pin in it – that is what followed: "Ness," she said. "I don't get it." Best friends are supposed to get everything, no matter how wacky the idea is. I can't say it didn't make me feel a little bit deflated, but I didn't take it personally. I just knew that one day I would be able to go back to her and say: "Now do you get it?" I felt our idea had potential, so I was going to pursue it no matter what anyone else thought.

I had a number of conversations with a few key contacts in the City to see if they saw a market for our website. I remember speaking to a well-known CEO of a leading recruitment firm who absolutely warned me off creating the site. She was full of doom and gloom in terms of the downturn and said that people would be more interested in saving their jobs than looking to learn new things. To us, the two things went hand in hand. If people were worried about their jobs, then they should be upskilling and networking to increase their chances of finding good new roles.

Less than a week after Stewart first built the prototype of the site, we jumped for joy as we went live on the internet for the world to see. When we checked who had joined up as members of WeAreTheCity, we could see that 10 people had completed their details and registered on the site. We cracked open the champagne to celebrate and checked their details. It turned out to be my mum, his dad, my cousins and few of the girls who helped out with our market research, but it didn't even matter. We had turned an idea and a few bits of A5paper into something real – something that just maybe would go on to help thousands of women achieve their aspirations.

As Stewart and I came up with our strategy, we believed there were three main things that WeAreTheCity could do to add value for women:

1. Promote all of the different female networks and their events to our female audience.

2. Provide a platform for female entrepreneurs and businesses to get their quality products and services to a large female demographic.

3. Provide a conduit for charities to reach high net worth women who could support them in their endeavours.

We had established that our site would help working women, and there was a huge element of social responsibility wrapped up in what we were about to create, which very much played to my desire to give something back in some form.

I had a renewed spring in my step going into work for the next few weeks as everything I was focused on as soon as I left the office every night was getting home to build more of WeAreTheCity with Stewart. My internet investigations had slowed down, and I had enough information to start getting out and about in the UK to try and persuade as many networks as I could to get on board with our idea.

I had one major fear. I knew that if I was going to make this work, I too had to get out there and do some networking myself. It was something I had never actively done; however, if this was to succeed, it was a fear I needed to overcome.

I remember the first event I attended. I walked in, checked in my coat and stood at the back of the room absolutely frozen. Awkward would be an understatement. How was I supposed to break into a conversation when these women were clearly in full flow? What was my opening line? What was my story, and what did I bring to the table by being here? I never knew how to leave a conversation that had obviously come to an end; I never knew how to lift a conversation if it fell silent. It was all so new to me and I was uncomfortable with it. In fact, at the first event I attended, I hadn't even remembered to take any business cards with me.

It took me a good six months before I could walk into a room and just join in as if it was my event. I had watched natural networkers work a room, and I sought advice from a woman called Heather White who I'd researched as one of two of the most experienced networking experts in the City (the other being Andy Lopata). I deliberately targeted one of her events, hoping that I could get to speak to her and find out the tricks she used to make networking easier. She told me a great story which is one that I share regularly to this day. Being only 5'2", Heather's greatest fear at a networking event is tall people. Her way of dealing with it is that whenever she enters a room full of people, the first person she approaches is the tallest person in the room. Her theory is that once her biggest fear is conquered, the rest is easy!

The more I networked at these various events, the better I got at it. Before I knew it, I was advising others how to overcome their confidence barriers and sharing the amazing benefits I was already recognising from meeting all these new people and learning lots of great new skills. I now have a tendency to round up newbies and people on their own in a room because I remember exactly how it felt. Before they know it, I'm giving them a master class in networking and soon they are on their way towards conquering their own fears.

Over the next few months, WeAreTheCity's membership grew to the point where we had over 100 members. We were issuing our newsletter every week asking our existing members to recommend 10 members in return for £20 worth of vouchers. It worked, and word soon started to spread around the City about our little site.

With each event I attended, I would approach the organisers and ask them if they wanted to be featured on WeAretheCity. At first they didn't understand why I would want to promote their activities for free. They couldn't get their heads around the fact that I just wanted to help other women like me and this was something I wanted to do because I felt passionate about it. Given that it was free promotion for them, they soon got over their confusion around my motives.

We asked our existing members to start writing for us or recommending us to other writers. We wanted to hear the stories that would benefit City women written by other women. We knew there would be lots of women out there who would have had experience with situations that would resonate with our audience or who were qualified to impart advice on a particular subject of interest. Our channels for content also grew as I networked my way around the City.

We started to see a significant number of bounced emails every time we sent out a newsletter. At first we suspected that this was happening because those women were changing roles. As it turned out, they weren't changing roles. This was mid-2008, and they were in fact losing their jobs because of the recession. This made me even more determined to put something in place that could help them.

By now WeAreTheCity had been live for several months, and we knew we needed to put ourselves on the map more formally. I had done enough talking, and it was time to show the City we meant business. We decided to do an official launch as a grand affair, right in the heart of the City, in the best venue our savings could afford. Prior to that, though, we thought it would be best to hold a pre-launch event as a test run.

Our pre-launch event was at a private members' club near the Royal Exchange by Bank tube station in the City. Our idea was to do something fun which we knew would attract a crowd, so we decided we would show women how to transfer their daytime office looks to night-time glam. We filled the club with over 100 women. With students from the Royal College of Fashion, stylists, top hairdressers and make-up artists from

Mac, we transformed women over the course of a couple of hours, fusing fashion and everything that is feminine alongside corporate networking. That event was a huge success and gave us confidence for our official launch.

On 15 September 2008 we held our official launch event. We hired the most prominent department store in the heart of London for a night of champagne, networking and fashion for over 250 of our members. As I approached the store, I could see hundreds of women queueing around the building. This event was going to be everything I had dreamed it would be. As I made my way through the crowd, I could not help but stand back and admire the glow of pink lights that illuminated the building and etchings of our high heeled logo etched on the store's windows. I could see the small team of stay-at-home mums that I'd hired for the occasion waiting for the doors to open in their WeAreTheCity uniforms. It was a truly magical moment.

I couldn't breathe for excitement as I picked up the local City newspaper the next day to see if we had made the headlines. There was our website's name and a half-page feature covering the event. We were the talk of the City, and for the first time in a long time I felt as if I had actually made a difference for all the right reasons. Stewart and I had taken this wine-induced sunbed idea and made it into something tangible in four months. We were giving women the opportunity to build support networks, and although both events we had run so far were 'softer' events, our plans were for more career-development orientated events to follow. I knew in my heart that I had found my calling, and this was the start of a particularly special period in Stewart's life and in mine.

The next event that followed was the one that established WeAreTheCity as a serious player. Through my connections, I had spoken with a US investment bank that wanted to run a large-scale networking event aimed at women. After meeting with them, they told me that they would take a chance on our website and make us their partner for the event if I could secure a hard-hitting speaker. We talked about the type of speaker they wanted and they mentioned Nicola Horlick. Nicola was known as the 'City Superwoman' given her high-flying career as a fund manager and role as the mother of six children. She had seen her fair share of ups and downs in the corporate world and definitely had a story that would draw a crowd and inspire women. I left the meeting wondering how on earth I would secure Nicola or anyone remotely similar with no budget for a speaker's fees. If I wanted to make an impression on my client, I knew I would have to find a way. I sat down the following Sunday and penned an email to Nicola. I had no idea what her email address was, neither did I know anyone who could facilitate an introduction. In my note I explained what WeAreTheCity was and asked if she would consider speaking for our little start-up. I spent half an hour guessing her email address and each time I tried to send my email, it would bounce back. Eventually I got it right, and as the email left my inbox, I sat back in my chair and prayed. Two weeks later, I was checking my Blackberry and there it was – a reply. In her email, she thanked me for inviting her to speak and stated she would be delighted to do so. I remember stopping in my tracks, looking up at the sky and mouthing 'thank you'.

The event with Nicola was an amazing success and she brought the house down with both her career and personal stories. After that event and the subsequent press coverage, we had no problem whatsoever convincing other corporates to sponsor or partner with us for events. Both Nicola and the US investment bank who gave us that chance back in 2008 really made a difference to our fledgling business, and to this day I honestly cannot thank them enough.

On the strength of our successful events, Stewart and I discussed how we would grow the site alongside our pressured day jobs. Given the economic downturn, we knew that company advertising budgets were being squeezed, and therefore income to the site would be slow. We couldn't hire the much-needed team that would have propelled the site's growth. We decided we would just go slow and do as much as we physically could outside of hours. Our plan was to build the brand over the next two to three years, grow our website traffic to a decent number and when the time was right, we would go after the large advertising clients who would be interested in promoting their services and products to our extensive female membership. We quickly realised that expanding the website and marketing ourselves as the 'go-to' site for women was going to cost more than expected. We agreed we would fund the site out of the spare cash we had managed to save over the past few years and income from Stewart's new contracting role. We didn't want a bank loan and we didn't want an investor – we felt that this was our baby and if we were going to mess it up, we only wanted to have ourselves to blame. In hindsight, we should have taken out a business loan, as we financed WeAreTheCity over the next four years via the most expensive form of credit: credit cards! I didn't feel quite as bad about that when I learned that leading clothing brand Jack Wills started exactly the same way and have now managed to turn themselves into a multi-million pound brand.

The world of finance and banking seemed to be falling to its knees as 2008 closed. Even the bank I was still working in was challenged. It wasn't long before the bars came down on spending and the layoffs began. Bit by bit, I watched my CTO's power diminish as all projects were put on hold. It quickly got to the point where we could barely order stationery without seeking special approval from the US or completing five forms. I knew it was only a matter of time before my CTO was moved to another role or they got rid of him entirely.

With the need to fund WeAreTheCity at the forefront of my mind, I decided that I would leave my secure job. It might not have seemed logical to give up a job where I was well-respected and probably still had quite an exciting future just as the recession was about to take its tightest hold. But I had my eye on what would happen next: work would still need to be done in many firms across the City but firms didn't want permanent headcount sitting on their books keeping their fixed costs high. I was betting that the world of contracting would be heating up. I also knew I could earn double my salary in the contract market, and not being a full-time employee would make me feel less guilty about building WeAreTheCity alongside my day job. It was a risky strategy, but I'd done enough homework to determine that this was a risk worth taking.

I put my CV out to the market with the very same contacts that had helped me secure my previous role a few years earlier. Within three weeks I was offered three contract roles at major investment banks. It was then just a case of choosing which one would fit in with my aspirations outside of work.

My boss was shocked when I resigned, in fact he asked me if I was nuts, quitting my job at such a volatile time in the market. I believed that by seizing opportunities when everyone else was holding back, I was getting a head start. Right before I left, my boss told me that the CEO of our business had said: "We have to let her go. But who knows, maybe one day we might be lucky enough to get her back." I couldn't have asked to leave on a better note.

Leaving that bank was closure in so many ways. I had joined the firm with incredible aspirations and had been through so much in the process of trying to realise all my dreams. It had been a journey of discovery and, in many ways, I didn't actually like what I found on a personal level. From a learning perspective, though, I couldn't have worked in a better place.

Out of the three contracting options I had managed to secure, I was convinced to join a particular bank by one of my recruitment agents. It turned out to be the very same bank where I had worked with Jake. They were merging with another bank, and the job I would be doing involved helping unpick the very projects I had helped to implement all those years ago.

I met the line manager over a coffee before I started. He was quiet and conservative. As I walked back from our meeting there was something in my gut that was questioning whether he was the sort of individual I would work well with. By now I had worked out that the person I worked for was as important to me as the job I was expected to perform. Since this was a contracting role, though, I felt that he and I were 'dating' as opposed to 'marrying', so I didn't think that getting a perfect fit was quite as crucial. That said, I wish I had listened to my gut instinct!

When I joined, every morning my new boss would acknowledge everyone else in his all-male team except me. Considering I was supposed to be his number two, I found this very odd. I also found him to be a closed book when it came to any form of communication. I have no issues with introverted people and I'll rein in my extrovert personality if I know I'm working with someone where we'll need to spend more time building a relationship due to our personality differences. But this guy was not making the slightest attempt to have any kind of relationship with me. I lasted just six months in the organisation – not even because of him, but more because the organisation had so many financial constraints I was virtually unable to perform my role properly. I sat with over 50 contractors who would show up at 9am and twiddle their thumbs all day until 5pm when they ran out of the door. Even the permanent staff were in a state of limbo as they watched their share price fall day by day and their pensions and savings being eaten away. I felt like I was going mad, and it was a madness that was getting to me even with the great income I was getting to fund my dream from the inflated day rate they were paying me. I questioned why I was actually sitting there allowing my brain to shrink when I could be elsewhere building my website and doing some good in the world.

I decided to leave. By now I had got quite good at resigning, having done it no fewer than six times! I explained the rationale behind my decision and that I felt the bank was wasting its money by having me and my team on site when the organisation was in such a state of flux. To his credit, he offered me the option of going part time until such time as the organisation was prepared to spend money and do more projects again. I declined politely even though it would have meant earning money for doing literally nothing – it was just not my style to do so.

Once my notice period was up, I was fully intending to take a bit of time out before I looked for my next contract. On my last day of work, a headhunter asked me to go for an interview at a leading asset manager. The job was a dream role from a PMO perspective: £200m transformation portfolio, the chance to implement a full-scale project methodology, global responsibility and recruitment of a team of 13 people. I would have been mad not to at least interview for it. The main problem was that it was a permanent role, which would have meant earning less than the contract roles and compromising my plan to financially support and spend more time on WeAreTheCity.

I went for the job interview regardless, as I like to think that all interviews are a good opportunity to meet new people and hone my interview skills

Thinking nothing more of it once I'd done the interview, I travelled to Spain for a break and to think about what I was going to do next. I had literally left my job on the Thursday, interviewed at the asset managers on the Friday and flown off to Spain on the Saturday. At 9am on Monday morning, my mobile rang. It was the headhunter about the asset management role. "Vanessa, they want you, like yesterday, and you can name your price!"

The price was less about the salary I might want and more about me taking a step back from WeAreTheCity. We were just at a point where we were really starting to get considerable interest in the website, both from members and potential advertisers. Not only would taking this role delay my grander plan, but I questioned whether I really wanted to go back into the fire when I was just on the cusp of getting out?

I was in two minds. The plus side of the interview process was that I had really connected with both heads of change who interviewed me, so if I did decide to join I knew that both bosses were definitely the right fit for me. I also liked the firm; it was a million miles away from the hard-core world of US investment banking I was used to, and from a cultural perspective it would be a much less aggressive environment. That said, the job they were hiring me for and their aspirations in terms of their change programme wouldn't be easy. The role ticked all my boxes in terms of a challenge, and the fact that the deliverables needed to be turned around in a short timeframe. I knew I could do it and do it well.

I procrastinated while they continued to dangle various compensation packages in front of me that were hard to refuse. The longer I was taking to make up my mind, the better it got. I wasn't actually delaying as a tactic to get a better package, I just really needed the time to think hard about my decision. If I took the role, I would be compromising what I now knew I really wanted to do, which was to build my site and work with women. I had yet another choice to make. Would it be a good year of putting the focus back on my career with little time for anything else, or pursuing my dream to give back and do something different? Decisions, decisions, decisions.

CONTENTMENT

Like everyone else around me, I had bills to pay, so the attraction of taking a few months off to focus on the website was very much hampered by the reality of my mortgage, childcare and other financial obligations. At the end of 2008 everyone was tightening their belts. Everywhere you looked, the press were stating that this was the start of what would be a five-year journey into the pits of a recession, and job losses and cuts would hit the City in a major way. They weren't wrong!

In the end I decided to accept the new job, hoping that the recession wouldn't be as long as the economists predicted. Time permitting, I would continue to plough my efforts into the website and network on the side, but ultimately work security had to come first as that was what was going to keep my household running. I anticipated staying at my new firm for about two to three years at most and hopefully within that time I'd be lucky enough to do a couple of different roles in that firm to broaden my experience. I was conscious of not staying longer than three years at any firm during the early part of my career and I had almost doubled my salary as a consequence; you earn more by moving to a new job than you do with incremental annual pay rises. If money is your driver, jumping jobs every two to three years early in your career is a decent strategy. I never understood the people who stayed with the same firm for 20 years and wondered why they weren't getting paid as much as peers who had come in from other companies!

When I arrived at my new role, the size of the change portfolio I was due to control shrank drastically; the economic crisis continued to deepen. The size of the portfolio actually decreased by over 80% from what the firm had originally planned as part of its transformation. To some extent, I think there were delusions of grandeur in their original numbers given the external environment. I was all for pushing forward when the rest of our competitors were pulling back; however, that figure would have been ambitious even for an asset manager who was three times our size.

The golden carrot, that huge portfolio, now looked more like a limp piece of celery, and both my team and I knew it. While we ended up having far less change to govern than anticipated, luckily there was still quite a bit of work to be done in terms of processes and building a future project methodology in preparation for when the change spend could rise in future years. We would be busy, but not as flat out as we had initially expected. I cleared out all contractors and consultants so that my permanent staff would reap the rewards of what we were about to build. I also didn't want the experience walking out of the door with any temporary people when we were done; I wanted what we were building to make the firm more sustainable.

There were more than a few shocks when I arrived in my new role. Not only was the portfolio shrinking, but 10 of the 13 people that I thought I was going to be recruiting for my team had already been hired. I was even more frightened when I found out a majority of them were women. I had only ever managed women for short periods of time over my career so I expected I was in for a steep learning curve. I was used to being able to take very technical and transactional approaches with large teams of men, but managing my all-new female team would require me to flex my style. It was clear that the direct 'just get it done' approach would not work with this group of women. I needed to build respect, trust and relationships with them, because without them on-side I was never going to be able to deliver on the commitments I had made in my interview. I reflected on my experience with Jake and the server migration. His model of getting the team on-side first and then introducing a few quick wins to drive momentum felt like it would be the appropriate approach for this role too.

While it was a very different environment from what I'd experienced previously, it did fulfil some stereotypical expectations of what would happen when a large group of women worked closely together. In the beginning as a new team we were still working things through, getting to know each other and establishing boundaries. They were a fabulous team, the crème de la crème in terms of PMO staff; however, as individuals they were all out to progress their careers and make their mark at the same time. I believe a bit of competition is healthy, and on occasions I encourage it – however, there are limits!

As we moved towards the forming stage, I knew I would have to mix my team up a little if we were to be as successful as I knew we could be. Over the course of the months that followed, I transferred new people into the team and focused my hires around more diverse individuals, a few of which were men. The dynamics in my all-female team changed almost immediately. They stopped competing against each other and joined forces to compete with the men. From a team psychology perspective it was fascinating to watch, especially as the guys in the team were almost oblivious to it.

The team settled in, and after nine months of hard work building the foundations that would allow change to be governed and controlled in the way we wanted it to be, we were firing on all cylinders. I truly believe we built one of the best PMO teams in the City, and to this day I wouldn't hesitate to rehire any of them. We worked hard, but we combined it with a lot of fun which reaped its rewards when the tough times came. I am a true believer in the old adage that a family that eats together stays together, so we had regular social events and time out of the office to get to know each other. When things went wrong, which they invariably did, we approached it as a team. No finger pointing, just joint accountability and joint recognition for all failures and achievements. That has always been my model as a leader.

When I arrived, I had asked for the PMO to be externally rated by a leading firm of PMO benchmarking experts, something I had done many times before. This is always a useful tool when going back to bosses later to show them how you have executed an improvement plan. I wasn't surprised that we were rated near the bottom quartile in terms of our processes and ability to govern change in the beginning; we were just starting out and nothing was in place. I told my team not to be disheartened, there was only one way our performance could go, and that was up. Within less than a year, when the second benchmarking exercise took place, not only had we moved up from the bottom, we were heading towards the top quartile of PMOs across the City. My team had pulled it off, and my work was done. We celebrated with a meal and a night out at a karaoke bar – little did I know that one of the women on my team had reached the final stages of a well-known reality TV talent show and had huge potential as a singer. The things you discover on nights out!

From the first day I arrived, I was scanning my team for my potential successor. I had been caught out on this one before, when my departure from one department was hampered by the fact that I had failed to train anyone up to take my place. Many leaders forget this important aspect of team building and get stuck in their roles for longer periods of time than they would like. I didn't just find one when I looked around this time, I found two. That would have been a big coup for any leader.

After running the PMO for almost a year and delivering half of the commitments I had made to my interviewers several months early, I felt that all-so-familiar 'itchy feet' feeling to move on to something else.

The COO (Chief Operating Officer) of the organisation had just left, and rumours of the new COO's arrival had already started to circulate. The incoming COO had been billed as a 'hatchet man' so the grapevine was alive with speculation.

We had seen a slightly dishevelled character in the office on and off for the past few weeks, but no one thought he could be the new COO. He looked more like he had just come off a farm than one of the slick, charismatic individuals that normally occupy such positions.

Of course it was him, and he was certainly not what any of us expected in any way. His brain entered the room long before his brand and ego did which was a rarity, based on what I had seen from previous leaders at his level. He stated up-front that he wasn't planning to fire anyone and he didn't intend to start fixing things that weren't broken. He was also very honest in terms of his current knowledge of our business.

His name was Jeremy, and it was very apparent that he came from outside the City and had never worked for an asset manager. He did have extensive experience in the insurance sector and, given that he had a brain the size of planet, it wasn't going to take him long to get up to speed. He was a true delivery-orientated individual and what he had come in to do was to help transform our organisation.

In our first meeting, when I was offering to help him settle into the company, I casually mentioned that I felt the reporting line of the current PMO was conflicted as it reported directly to the organisation it was supposed to be governing, thus losing its independent view. I shared a minimal amount of detail about organisational designs I had worked with in the past, most of which had their PMOs reporting directly to the COO or to a transformation director.

I was in limbo in terms of a new boss, so although it was cheeky, I thought I would make my pitch early, remembering my mum's words that if you don't ask, you don't get. I had prepared my verbal business case before I approached him, and I was succinct in terms of the reasons why and how this would benefit the organisation. The practice I had gained in previous roles in pitching my case for change had prepared me well. He moved our reporting line that very week and there began my relationship with one of the most unusual and academically brilliant individuals I have ever met in my career. He was a gentleman who would continue to place pieces into the complex puzzle that was my corporate career well into the future.

Jeremy and I were massively different in terms of background but that wasn't an issue when working alongside him. I was the girl who so far had quit more jobs than she cared to mention, whereas he had a 10-year track record in the same company, running some of the group's largest subsidiaries. I came from a less than academic background, whereas he had an education that would rival any Oxford scholar's. We were worlds apart, and yet somehow we connected. I had the people skills he openly admitted he lacked and the organisational skills he needed to get a mountain of things done, and I knew I would be an asset to him, even if it was on an interim basis. It wasn't long before helping him out above and beyond my day job turned into a request to work for him full time as his business manager. It was an opportunity and challenge I accepted enthusiastically.

Not only was he a joy to work for, but he continued to give me stretch tasks, mostly because he just assumed I could do them. I never let him down, even if it involved my normal process of reading books and learning at home. However, given my extensive networking over the past couple of years, I now had a raft of individuals I could call upon for advice. I truly felt that I had a seat at his leadership table. He would listen to my views and ultimately let me play a part in shaping our new team and our goals. I had found another diamond in the rough who was prepared to let me just run with things and who I was happy to let shape me as a future leader.

Jeremy was extremely supportive of WeAreTheCity and my endeavours to help other women in their careers. He wholeheartedly encouraged it, often giving me time off to speak at events and represent my company from a diversity perspective. He appreciated that I had a young family and would often tell me off if I worked late or came into work immediately after I had travelled overseas. His approach to such things was hugely refreshing after my experiences in my previous firm where I would fly in from New York on the overnight flight, shower at Heathrow and be at my desk the same morning by 9am because that's what was expected!

Jeremy also suggested that if I wanted to work from home on the odd day I was welcome to do so. Having worked with global companies most of his career, he'd been managing remote teams all over the world. He didn't need me to be tied to my desk all day, every day, and if working from home made it easier for me to get things done, then that was my decision. I didn't need to seek permission to do so. At last I was being treated like a grown-up!

Jeremy totally understood the need for balance and that if you give back to your staff in ways that make them feel that life is not just about work, you get happier and more dedicated employees. On the flipside, when times were tough and I did need to work late, or things came up workwise at the weekend, of course I would gladly spring into action. The relationship was very much based on give and take and was similar to how I had run my own teams in the past.

Jeremy was an extremely perceptive individual when it suited him. Generally our working day was fairly transactional. I would take what I needed to get my job done, he would take what I had produced in order to do some of his job. We did make time for small talk, but it was generally after my recitation of what we needed to do for the week ahead and not before. I would often rattle through our to-do list and at the end of the conversation he would say with raised eyebrows: "Oh, and by the way, good morning Vanessa, how are you today?" – his way of reminding me it wasn't always about cracking the whip!

After working for Jeremy for over a year, he asked me one morning why, in a number of our conversations, I had referred to the fact that I hadn't gone to university. He wanted to know why it bothered me so much. I explained that I used to feel quite intimidated by some of my previous investment banking peers because they had been lucky enough to study for degrees and benefit from a university education and I hadn't, and somehow I had always felt that this had held me back in some way. I also mentioned that this was probably more about my own assumptions and insecurities than anyone in the past deliberately making me feel uncomfortable about my lack of a degree. There was a natural assumption in our sector that anyone who had got to a mid to senior level had benefited from such an education. I recounted the amount of times earlier in my career when I had been asked quite innocently what university I had attended, and for years I would just mumble and change the subject. I then went through a cheeky stage where I would answer: "The university of hard knocks and the school of life" which generally got the message across that I hadn't gone and didn't want to talk about it.

It really did bother me that I hadn't gone to university. There was a part of me that wished things had been different when I left school and that I could have continued my education. There were so many roles I hadn't applied for in the early days when the job specifications said 'university educated' or 'degree essential'. On more than one occasion, I knew I had the experience to do the job, but those words would always put me off. I wonder how many companies still lose out on interviewing talented individuals who just never got the chance to continue their education. There is a lesson in there somewhere for talent recruiters; if you always do what you have always done, you will always get what you have always got! If companies want to enhance their talent pool, they need to do away with some of these archaic rules or they stand to lose out in the war for talent.

Jeremy told me in the nicest of ways that he thought I had a bit of a chip on my shoulder about my education. In his opinion he didn't think I needed to go back and plug the gap, but if I felt it was an issue then I should do something about it. He said that he would support me by helping me find the right programme.

During the same period I was also asked to sit on a panel at a women's event to speak about my career. The organisation that was running the event asked me for a short biography. I didn't have a bio, I had a fairly extensive CV but that was about it. I confessed to them that I didn't have one and asked if they could send me bios from some of the other panellists so I could write something similar for consistency. The bios from the other panelists all cited PhDs and Master's degrees. That little person on my shoulder – you know, the one that kicks your confidence – started to tell me that I didn't deserve to be on the same panel with these people, as I hadn't achieved as much as they had in terms of educational background. One half of me was saying it didn't matter, the other half of me was saying it absolutely did! I sat down to write the bio with the others sat there staring up at me, and after 30 minutes of staring at a blank piece of paper I wrote 'I'm just me' as that was exactly how I felt. How could it be that after all I had gone through and achieved that these insecurities continued to plague me? The education issue wasn't my only hang-up either; in fact, behind the brand I had started to build with the decent CV and the confident exterior, there were a few more aspects of 'me' that I still felt needed improving.

I realised that I actually did want to go back to complete my education, it was unfinished business. I was going to go back to a university or business school of some sort to prove to myself that I could do academic learning, and I was going to plug some of the gaps in my corporate learning at the same time. I was going to obtain those precious words for my future bio and CV, I wanted to say that I'd done it and I had the t-shirt. University educated, job done. I had rarely read bios of CEOs or COOs that didn't start with their back-catalogue of education, so why not right what I perceived to be wrong with my own educational story? It certainly couldn't hurt!

I cannot tell you how many people told me not to bother. They all saw that I had got to a fantastic place in my career on the strength of being good at my job and my own tenacity. What was the point in returning to such a pressured learning environment at the age of 37 when I was already in a senior role? The only person who actively understood why I wanted to do it was Jeremy. Even Stewart didn't get it. I had often envied Stewart's stories of university life and then going off to backpack around the world. I wanted to have at least half of that story. The travel part was going to have to come at a later date!

I started to investigate business schools all over the City to find out what they offered corporate women. From a London perspective, I looked at Cass Business School, Cranfield, Henley and Ashridge, all of which had amazing corporate offerings. One business school caught my eye because of its stunning reputation and successful alumni: University of Chicago Booth Business School, conveniently located very close to my office.

I looked through their various offerings with Jeremy's help, including their MBA programme. The MBA would have meant a compromise too far in terms of cost and time away from work and the family. What they did offer which looked ideal was an Accelerated Development Programme (ADP) for corporate leaders as part of their Executive Education offering. It contained all of the MBA subjects and could be done over six months, and it would only take me out of the office for half a day once a month. The rest of the time would be made up at weekends. The only other time commitment involved would be reading the case studies before class. As with any decision in our household, I discussed whether the time commitment was achievable with Stewart, as I knew I would be losing a couple of weekends with him and the children. As usual, he was happy to support me because he knew how much plugging my gaps academically meant to me, even if he still didn't necessarily understand why.

I interviewed at the school, opening the interview with the dean by stating that I probably didn't have the academic entry qualifications I needed to be on the programme, but I did have over 20 years of experience and a diverse approach to business on my side. He didn't take much convincing and welcomed me to Chicago Booth.

The course itself covered a myriad of topics including leadership, corporate finance and financial accounting. I knew which subjects I would be engaged in and which ones were likely to send me to sleep. I have a real aversion to learning things that don't interest me and have to try twice as hard to focus on the detail and absorb what I am being taught if I deem the subject boring. The finance modules were my biggest fear, but I knew that particular fear needed to be faced. I hoped it would be a way of overcoming my number demons which only seemed to appear when a previous boss told me I couldn't add up. He said it because he was a qualified accountant and I wasn't. Those kinds of comments, especially when they come from someone you actually admire, tend to stick in your head, and before you know it you can convince yourself that whoever said it was right.

Despite being wonderful at maths at school, doing the numbers wasn't a skill that I had used much in my career as I always had people around to do it for me. I was aware that in order to progress it was important that I understood how to interpret a profit and loss (P&L) statement and company accounts. I also knew that most of my previous bosses had P&L experience, so the first step for me would be to learn this so called 'dark art' and then put it into practice at some future point in my career.

I loved being at Chicago Booth and used to count down the days to my next stint of learning. On my first day, I arrived in the large auditorium and took my seat at the back, a true testament as to where I felt I belonged in the room! The first professor told us a story about one of his first lectures when he'd attended Yale. He too had taken a seat at the back of the hall. His Yale professor approached him and asked him if he always intended to take a back seat in life, or did he want to move to the front and compete with the rest of the pack? The story really resonated with me. I made sure at the start of my second lecture that I was firmly seated at the front of the auditorium!

My class at Chicago Booth was made up of 30 people – some COOs and other senior players from large organisations. There were a few CEOs who owned their own successful businesses. I had no problems integrating or networking with them, given the skills I'd picked up over the past few years. I found it very easy to break into conversations and, as Heather White would put it, work the room.

The diversity of backgrounds in the room on our programme was amazing. We represented 20 different countries and together we challenged subjects and debated issues as a group. It was obvious that this would be a learning experience that went far beyond what we were being taught academically.

I completed the course and received my honour as well as a glowing reference from the dean. I remember digging out my meagre bio and updating it. 'Vanessa Vallely studied at the University of Chicago Booth.' It was a great feeling. Regardless of whether I was ticking a box for me or for my doubters, I had said I would go to university, and now I'd done it!

Going back to academic learning was a wonderful experience and opportunity, and I don't regret the time investment one little bit. What I do regret is how I allowed myself to feel so inadequate for so many years, because in the grand scheme of things, it was just a line on a piece of paper to say that I had attended and been taught at university level. It was an important achievement for me personally , but to all intents and purposes it really didn't change anything dramatically given my extensive experience in my various corporate roles.

While studying on the ADP I was still working full time with the odd day from home and continuing to build WeAreTheCity with what little time I had left. Some nights Stewart and I would stay up way beyond midnight as we were designing a new section of the site or planning our next event. By now we had in the region of 300,000 hits and around 15,000 unique visitors per month, as well as 100 female writers and over 5,000 members. My quest to be the biggest website for working women in the City still held firm, and I wanted to double those numbers over the next two years.

Now that I was active on the City networking circuit, I was being asked to speak at events and forums for women all the time. I felt that my role was to inspire women and make them realise that with a bit of support and knowledge they could achieve their career or entrepreneurial goals. I would happily share my story and whatever else I was qualified to talk about, either for free or for a small donation to one of the charities I was supporting. I was starting to be recognised in the City as a go-to person for female development opportunities, connections and advice. It was yet another great feeling of accomplishment, given the fact I wouldn't have stepped near a women's network a year earlier.

It was mid-June of 2009 when a lady by the name of Suzanne Doyle Morris, author of the book *Beyond the Boys' Club* and one of the panellists I was lucky enough to collaborate with earlier that year, called me to say she wanted to nominate me for an award from Women in Banking and Finance (WIBF). I was already familiar with WIBF as they were one of the first networks I investigated when I started WeAreTheCity. They were also one of the very first networks that agreed to let us promote their events to the members of WeAreTheCity. A beautiful partnership was formed that still holds firm to this day.

I knew of the annual awards ceremony as I had been invited to attend as a guest the previous year by the then chair, Christine Lawrence. It was an electric atmosphere at the beautiful Dorchester Hotel, watching all of these amazing women collect their awards, and I loved seeing the excitement created by their male and female supporters, all of whom had come together to celebrate the nominees' achievements.

The award Suzanne was nominating me for was Women's Champion. I was slightly taken aback at even being nominated when up until quite recently I'd been anything but a women's champion or role model. I was very emotional on that call with Suzanne, as I was so happy to be thought of as someone in the City community who was actively giving back to women, especially by someone who was very highly regarded by so many herself.

After setting up WeAreTheCity and making my way around the City to all of the different networks and events, it was clear to me that what was making me whole as an individual wasn't just about my corporate career anymore. I loved the corporate world and felt comfortable there, but I also had this new career outside of work that filled me with equal if not greater passion. I honestly felt that I had the best of all worlds at this point: a great boss, a job I loved, balance and harmony at home, a website that was going from strength to strength, I was helping others, plus I was getting the opportunity to share my story in the hope that it would inspire or motivate the next generation of corporate women.

Prior to attending the WIBF annual awards ceremony, I had been asked to speak about my career at a small event run by an organisation called the City Speakers Club. The City Speakers Club was a small networking group headed by an amazing lady who has since retired. Even though I'd been speaking more often at various events, I always found the whole process to be a tense time. It wasn't any concerns about the content of my story or my presentation style, it was yet another of those hang-ups that surfaced every time I was on a stage: my accent and grammar.

My concerns about my accent had started back in the days when I would train graduates as part of my role as an IT trainer. I used to dread the odd grammatical slip-up or dropping my H's or T's, more through the speed at which I spoke rather than anything else. I have always been immensely proud of my cockney background, and while I appreciate that my London accent comes with that, I was acutely aware that there were people who had judged me and my capabilities the moment I opened my mouth and East End came out. One person in particular used to pull me up regularly in mid conversation and sometimes in the presence of other colleagues as well, taking great joy in correcting my pronunciation or choice of certain words. I vowed one day that when I had the time and money, I would invest in elocution lessons just so I could switch it on in situations where I felt it was needed. While I wanted to tell the world: "I am what I am and I'm not changing for anyone and if you are judging me based on an accent, then that's your problem," I knew that it really didn't work that way, and I would feel better if, after a few lessons, it could stop being something I worried about. I didn't want to give anyone the opportunity to judge me on the basis of my accent. I wanted to be measured by the advice I was imparting, not by how my words were pronounced. It is such a shame that prejudices against accent still exist in modern times, however, in pockets they do!

I spoke at the City Speakers Club and then asked for help from its founder, Charmian Ingham, a thespian and voice coach to radio presenters and actors alike. I said that I needed her help to address a few confidence issues I had with my accent and suggested she could liken our coaching sessions to Eliza Doolittle from the story My Fair Lady, an analogy she found hilariously funny. She assured me I was no Eliza. Within weeks she had me doing all sorts of weird and wonderful exercises with my voice, learning how to project and pronounce words

I had struggled with for years. The most important thing she taught me was to slow down when I speak. My mouth goes as fast as my brain, and I could not assume that everyone in my audience would absorb what I was saying at the same speed. By the time I finished our programme I was reciting Queen Elizabeth I's speech to the troops fighting the Spanish Armada in a dialect that would have rivalled royalty. Here was another box ticked. There was still this big part of me that felt conflicted, even resentful, that yet again I'd had to change the way I was in order to be accepted by a few individuals in the corporate world.

I did actually bump into one of the people who had been a regular offender in correcting my speech in public. When I told him that I had taken a few elocution lessons, he was absolutely shocked and appalled that what he perceived to be day-to-day banter when he'd done that had made me feel inadequate in some way. He continued to apologise for months after I'd told him, despite me telling him in the meantime that it was OK and he hadn't been the first but he would be the last!

It had been a few months since Suzanne's call and I had almost forgotten about my nomination for the WIBF award. Out of the blue I received an email telling me that out of hundreds of entries, I had been shortlisted for the Women's Champion award and was one of three finalists. Regardless of whether I won or not at this point, I felt like a winner. I couldn't believe that I would be one of those nominees that I'd seen everyone cheer on a year before, and I was speechless.

I attended the award ceremony that year accompanied by two tables of friends and colleagues from work. I was so proud to also have both my mum and dad there. I will never forget the train journey to London that morning, I was so nervous. That little imposter who lives on my shoulder was telling me how I didn't deserve to share the same stage with some of these amazing women, but there I was, all dressed up and ready to go anyway.

I had managed to build quite a network on the women's circuit and I knew on this special day they would all be there to support me. The amount of texts and emails I received in the run-up to the awards was incredibly touching, and actually showed me that I had much more support than I'd ever imagined. I should have taken time out to enjoy the day, however if you have ever been in that situation where you are waiting for your name to be called, you know it's extremely nerve-wracking. All of your supporters are looking at you, rooting for you, and you don't want to let them down by not winning.

And I didn't win, but I was still just happy to part of such an amazing experience and I truly believed this was a turning point. I had been recognised and that was way beyond what I had expected. All of the fabulous women in my category had been clearing the path for other women for years, setting up networks within their firms and mentoring other women. When I looked at what I had done over the last couple of years it didn't quite compare to their achievements – not just yet, I said to myself, but soon.

The lady who won Women's Champion that year turned out to become one of my dearest friends – Heather Melville, founder of the Focused Women's Network at Royal Bank of Scotland. She was an incredibly deserving winner who had built her internal corporate network with zero budget from nothing to one of the most successful women's networks in the corporate space, providing events and growth opportunities for several thousands of female members, all alongside her day job as a regional sales director. She is a role model if ever there was one, and someone who is still very close to my heart.

A stellar six months followed, balancing my corporate role, travelling abroad when I needed to, ensuring I had quality time at home with the children and Stewart, building the website, speaking at events and growing my extensive network. I would often meet people before work, for 30 minutes at lunchtime and then again on my way home. These were individuals that others in my network were now connecting me to or whom I had met as they were in the audience at one of my speaking events. I would meet anyone I could with a view to helping them with either advice or connections or both. I can't say it wasn't (or isn't still) tiring, but I get an immense sense of pleasure in connecting people and creating what I like to call 'magic'. It is a wonderful feeling to know that the 30 seconds you took to pen an introductory email to connect two people has enabled them to go on to achieve great things. I get to hear lots of success stories about what my connections have led to, and that makes the effort I put in extremely worthwhile.

It was the end of 2009, and everything appeared to be in its box. I was very excited to be given the opportunity by Jeremy to travel to India to meet with a couple of business process outsourcers. Jeremy had extensive experience in the outsourcing space, however it wasn't something I could buy into from a business perspective as I hadn't experienced it or seen it with my own eyes. Given the projects we were due to run at work, Jeremy suggested I should go and find out just how amazing the country and its people are, he wasn't wrong. I was there for a couple of days when I received a call from a UK number, a headhunter. I told him I was in India but he proceeded to explain that he was working on a senior role for one of the biggest banks in the City. I do still always listen to headhunters or recruitment agents even when I've no intention of moving roles in case the role they are pushing may not suit me but it may suit another individual within my network. I also always found the headhunters and recruiters to be useful contacts for lots of things. This particular headhunter had actually been consistently staying in touch with me by phone and via LinkedIn. We exchanged a few emails where I made it quite clear that I had no intention whatsoever of moving roles because I had found a job in a firm I loved and I would probably stay for at least another year or so.

This headhunter, much to his credit, was fairly persistent, and he hit a sweet spot in terms of my time when he called while

I was sitting in an airport en route to the UK. I engaged in a much more detailed conversation with him because I had time to kill, and much to my surprise I was quite interested in what he had to say. The role he was peddling was a chief operating officer for IT transformation, one of twelve COO roles across a bank's 10,000 IT professionals. Yes, this was indeed the big job. This was the one I had been after all those years ago when I was in the role that almost broke me. We continued the conversation a month later back in the UK, and purely out of recognition for his tenacity I agreed to go for a coffee with him to discuss the role further.

We met in one of London's most iconic settings to talk through the job description. I immediately connected with him as an individual, which is a must for me in a headhunter. If I am putting my next career choice in the hands of another person, they have to understand how I tick as a person and not just put me forward for a role because it looks like I fit on paper. The headhunter was brutally honest about the role and said it would be a challenge. The role was reporting to an up-and-coming executive who had already started to make a name for himself within this particular bank; the headhunter didn't tell me much more than that at the time. After several conversations, I gave in and agreed to go through the interview process, telling myself that I was doing it for experience and telling him that I needed quite a bit of convincing if I was to leave the job I loved and, above all, Jeremy. For the first time in my career, I actually felt as if I was betraying my boss by even talking to a headhunter.

It had been a while since I had last interviewed, and I looked at the whole process as an experience and an opportunity to be taken out of my comfort zone. I knew it was always good to see what was out there when you never know exactly what could be round the corner, the same reason why your CV should always be up to date as well. I admit that going through the interview process was a bit of ego boost too. This headhunter had pursued me for many months by now, and I started to think that if I really wanted to, I could potentially land this role and the long-awaited 'chief of something' title.

Over a three-month period, I went for more than 10 competency-based interviews, which is ridiculous by anyone's standards. Initially I wasn't that fussed at the amount of time it was taking, given that I'd already been dealing with this bank's recruiters for well over six months. It was never going to be a quick process and even if I did decide to move, they would have to add on the additional three months for my notice period. There was no way I would try to get out of my notice period; I refused to consider leaving Jeremy without support. If I did leave, I would need to find my replacement and do a proper handover so as to ensure that nothing fell through the gaps when I left. A control freak until the end, as ever!

I knew this new position was a very senior role, and even at the point of interview six I still wasn't convinced that this was the right route for me to take. Once again I was risking everything I had built, including my life balance. My gut instinct was that I should not continue interviewing beyond that point, but for some strange reason – ambition perhaps – I chose to ignore it.

During my interviews there were individuals who were warning me of certain challenges I would face if I were to take the role. I had been forewarned going into the interviews that there would be people who were part of my interview process who might try to put me off the role. This was a total game and, to be honest, I really didn't know who to trust. I should have realised that if there were these kinds of crazy politics and mind games at the interview stage, the actual day-to-day culture there would only be worse.

I also broke another of my fundamental rules about getting to know the person I'd be working for prior to accepting the job. In my defence, I had asked for additional meetings, but they were cancelled several times due to travel. The emails I received were always apologetic and welcoming. They also arranged for me to dine with a member of the exec as part of the interview process. They wanted me in the role, that was obvious, and they were rolling out the red carpet and dangling financial carrots to secure me. I was doing my best not to get pulled into the hype, but it was extremely hard to ignore.

I made it abundantly clear throughout the entire interview process that I planned to continue to run WeAreTheCity and that I had commitments to progressing the careers of women through the networks and my own endeavours, thinking that the bank might be put off by my split commitments. They weren't. In fact, both the HR folks and my new boss were hugely supportive. I also made it clear that I would need to work from home on the odd occasion too, as I now took my children to school and picked them up once a week and I wasn't prepared to compromise on that if I moved from my existing role. They agreed to that too. I think I could have asked for the world with a cherry on top at that point and they would have given it to me, they just wanted me to accept the role. My internal alarm bells should have been ringing to at least make me wonder why they seemed so desperate and willing to cave in on every point.

I was officially given the role when I was in Poland on a team offsite. Ridiculous as it sounds, I remember leaving dinner and taking the call, only to return to the table feeling almost unfaithful to the leadership team, Jeremy and the firm. However, there was another side of me that knew enough to know that I could not let my loyalty get in the way. This was a business decision on my part. If any of my male colleagues were considering the same offer, they would be in the throes of exiting by now. I was also acutely aware that when push comes to shove, we corporate workers are just numbers stored in a HR system. If hard times hit, which I had no doubt they would, it would be a numbers game and my loyalty to either Jeremy or the firm would count for nothing.

When I received my official offer letter, I took Jeremy out for a glass of wine to break the news. I didn't expect him to try to counter-offer, but I knew he would be disappointed. I ran our team's finances and I knew that the package the other bank was offering was way out of our league, even well above what we paid some of our directors. My new company had even pledged to buy out my bonus in order to get me to agree to take the role early. Jeremy looked down at his wine glass, almost speechless for a minute or so, before he said: "It's going to pain me to lose you, but I can't match that offer. If it's an opportunity you wish to go for and it does look amazing, go for it, and if it doesn't work for whatever reason and I still have opportunities here, you know the door is always open and I would gladly have you back."

Part of me felt so sad and so disloyal. I was almost wishing he would come up with reasons why I shouldn't take the role, and yet the other part of me, the old C-suit-craving career nut that I thought I had buried for a while, was massively excited at the prospect of being a key player, and above all being back in the real banking game. That said, I knew there would be some massive compromises, even with the terms I had laid out.

As usual I had discussed the proposition with Stewart and had also involved the kids because I knew it would impact them too. They were old enough to have opinions, and I valued them. Stewart was now extremely successful in his own corporate career and had no intention of moving anywhere soon, therefore from a stability perspective I had the green light to move roles. Stewart said he would support me whatever I chose to do, with the caveats that I was absolutely sure of what I was letting myself in for, had checked to make sure I understood just how big the role was and whether I felt I could work with my new boss. He knew that I had taken a back seat for a while and I think he had also started to think that I had given up my desires to rule the corporate world in some way. Up until this point, I'd almost thought exactly the same thing.

While all of this was going on I had also been awarded a place on the Financial News list of Top 100 Rising Stars in the City, EMEA and Africa. It was my first official accolade for my corporate career. I attended the awards ceremony in Mayfair with Stewart. As we took in the ambience of what was a stunning venue, I started to go off about my insecurities again about whether I deserved to be there and so on. Stewart turned to me and said: "For once, can you just enjoy the moment without questioning it? You got here through your passion and drive, your ability to survive against the odds and the fact you never give up. Just enjoy your champagne and celebrate your own achievements."

As we left Mayfair when the event was over, my head was full of questions about the unknown ahead. Could it be that things were pointing me back to the world of a full-on corporate life? Would it be different this time around given what I had learned from my previous roles? Would this new organisation really give me the balance I needed to do it all? Perhaps my new boss was the next Jeremy, Jake or Roy and I could finally place the last piece in the puzzle. Perhaps, perhaps, perhaps....

THE TIPPING POINT

As much as I fought it, I couldn't resist the lucrative package and the lure of the banking promised land. I was confident that this time it was on my own terms and for my own reasons. As I signed the acceptance letter, I drew comfort from the fact that by taking my COO role I was contributing to what was my wider, more strategic career plan. I had vowed never to go back to the testosterone-filled world of banking at a senior level unless someone was prepared to pay me a significant amount of money to do so, and this is exactly what the company was offering to do.

Before accepting the role, I spent half a day with Stewart mapping out my strategy and goals. Planning in cycles was taught to me by a former boss years ago, and it is something I have practised ever since for my own life as well as for business activities. I plan for three separate two-year periods at any one time. The first two years is my short term, years three and four are the medium term, and years five and six are the long term. Once I am in the long term, the cycle starts again. I was also taught to build shorter term, three to six month deliverables into my two-year plans as a way of keeping motivated. Three-month deliverables tend to work for me as it is a long enough period of time in which to do something tangible, but short enough to feel that I have achieved something. I have learned and often advised others that without plans or stakes in the ground to signpost your success, you are effectively lost without a map. I go on to explain how you put your own plans into action later in the book.

Short term, I planned to work at my new firm as COO for no longer than two years. I knew if I worked for them for two years I could earn enough to pay off all of WeAreTheCity's set-up costs which were mounting on credit cards, and then over time change my career to something I found more fulfilling.

That meant that mid-term, post my COO role, I would continue to grow WeAreTheCity and my other businesses while making money from a number of short-term interim positions. Long term, my utopian ideal would be to have more of a portfolio career.

A portfolio career by definition is holding a variety of positions at the same time. I was thinking about a portfolio career that still played to my experience, but for the long term it needed to be more about all my passions. I saw that a large proportion of that portfolio career would be spent giving my time to a variety of causes, including supporting corporate women, youth progression, charities and social enterprises. My hope is that I would generate my main income via WeAreTheCity and other business interests. If I could achieve that, it would feel like a fitting end to a 25-year corporate climb. It was becoming clearer that my definition of success had started to change, and this new COO role was probably going to be the last in terms of big ticket bank roles on my corporate CV. I was comfortable with the fact that I would need to serve another few years in the system if I was to move closer towards my eventual goals, which were more about giving than receiving.

While I would often daydream about a job where my role was purely about networking, mentoring young girls, inspiring the young who don't believe in all they can be, and motivating those mid-career types who just want to give up, I know that no such job exists, so my plan over time was to create it.

Over the past few years, alongside Stewart I had managed to build a business in WeAreTheCity that would ultimately contribute to my eventual exit plan. We had already started to see small revenues in terms of advertising and the site was now covering its own costs and leaving a bit of profit. By this point, we had approximately 8,000 members, 500,000 hits per month and around 40,000 unique visitors. We had started to chase the tails of the other major City sites, and sooner or later I knew that we would stand toe-to-toe with them and earn the advertising revenues that they were earning. It would just take time and a little more investment – investment that my new salary would cover.

Apart from being a little excited about my new role, I knew that taking it would be a challenge, both in terms of the organisation I was going to work for and managing my own time. When I take on a role, I like to throw myself into it and give it my absolute all, but I knew I would need to keep myself in check as I now had double the commitments I had a couple of years back. My biggest pledge to myself was that I had to find the balance between work and home life, and this meant ensuring I spent enough time with my friends and family. After almost losing my support network once there was no way I would be doing it again. My family comes first, end of story.

I knew within two weeks of joining the firm that it didn't feel right. I didn't feel right! That voice in my gut, the feeling of anxiety and reality of what two years would actually feel like finally dawned. I tried to talk myself out of it – if I was to achieve everything I wanted then I needed to take a few deep breaths and 'man up' as one of my old bosses would put it. I had taken the job and now I had to give it my best shot.

I was trying to work out what wasn't sitting right, what was my gut instinct reacting to? My goal forever had been to be a chief operating officer then a chief information officer and over time get a seat on the executive team. It was all pointing in the right direction. The achievement actually made me feel trapped – trapped by my own success and now the reliance on that level of pay. There is so much truth in the saying 'be careful what you wish for as you might just get it'. Now that the reality of the COO role was in front of me, I realised I really, really didn't want it.

Week after week, I would join the sea of 3,000 people trying to shuffle through the automated gates into my building, enduring the tube-like squeeze to get into the lift, desperately trying to ignore the little voice in my head that popped up frequently saying: 'You know you don't belong here anymore, why don't you just do what makes you happy?' Day after day, I was searching internally for the girl I used to be back in my days of US investment banking, the one who ran to work every morning and had a passion so deep for the corporate world that nothing and no one would get in the way of the job she needed to do, not even her own value system. As deep as I looked, I just couldn't find her.

Every day over the next four months I put as much effort as I could into building my new team. Bit by bit, I was gaining the trust of my stakeholders and peers while I was tackling significant issues that had been left unattended for far too long. From my perspective I was bedding in well, and from the feedback I was receiving it sounded like almost everyone else felt the same way. I believed everyone assumed I was happy and that I was in the job for the long haul, but behind closed doors this couldn't have been further from the truth.

As I mentioned previously, my own internal alarm bells had started ringing midway through my 13 hours of interviews. My main concern was that I hadn't got to know my line manager as well as I would have liked during the interview process. There were a number of other warning signs that I should have taken more notice of, like the fact that I was told to ignore any warnings about individuals or the organisation by those who were interviewing me. At the time, I just put this down to the normal politics that exist at a senior level, but my own external network were telling me that the organisation was not in a good place and wouldn't be for the next couple of years. One person even went so far as to recite the names of eight high-profile women who had joined the organisation and promptly left within six months. That should have made me run for the hills – but no, I thought I would be the one to break the mould. I am laughing at myself as I write, because I actually remember saying "It will be different for me" – how blinkered! What would make me so special? I ignored my own rules, I ignored my network, and against everyone's advice I joined the firm anyway. If I could go back and kick myself, believe me I would, several times!

I realised that the rumblings from my network were true. The organisation was in a state of flux, but that shouldn't have been that much of an issue because there is a great deal of opportunity to be had when organisations are struggling or going through major change. The biggest issue for me in my new role was that my boss and I were a complete mismatch. It wasn't his fault and I don't think it was mine either – it was just a personality thing.

I remember spending a few days in Spain on holiday deliberating whether to ride it out or leave. I was loath to give in, but the more I thought it through, the more I knew I had to go. The day after I returned from Spain I went in to see my boss who then told me that his job was being moved to another part of the organisation and he wanted me to come with him, and I would be expected to travel extensively. It was the perfect opportunity to share my own news that I had absolutely no desire to move, in fact the only place I was going was to human resources to hand in my notice. I remember walking up the corridor towards HR, and I suddenly couldn't contain my grin. It was the first time I had felt happy in that building and that told me I was doing the right thing.

I chose to walk away on this occasion for a number of reasons, which cumulatively carried more weight than my pay check and my title there.

I didn't actually want a chief position anymore. I didn't want the politics, I didn't want to spend time with the dog-eat-dog people who often operate at that level, and above all I didn't want all the crap that came with the fight for acceptance. I was prepared to be in a job that supported individuals who aspired to the things that I used to aspire to, as I felt I could guide them with the lessons I had learned and help to make them successful. All I wanted now was to return to a normal head of department job that was senior enough to bring about change and deliver to the organisation I worked for, but below the level of politics, egos and posturing that goes on at the top of the house in so many corporate organisations.

Luckily, my former boss Jeremy had stayed in my life as my advisor throughout my less than ideal experience as COO. He would often ring me up with a feeble excuse for a conversation that was really more about finding out how I was getting on in my new role. He ended each call by telling me that the door was always open at my old company should I ever choose to go back. I had no issue with going back, but my preference was to go back to a different challenge and a new role. True to his word, the moment he found out I was planning to leave he offered me exactly what I wanted and part-time as well. I believe that there are some people that the universe places in your life for a reason, and for me Jeremy is and will always be one of them.

On the whole, I'd been really lucky in my career, as I'd taken a lot of pretty big risks over time and most of them had worked out in my favour. My view was that when gambles don't pay off, you take stock, think about the learning, dust yourself off and put your heels of steel back on, because life invariably goes on. As much as I felt bruised by what had happened, when I looked at the situation through a positive lens I realised that I had actually ended up exactly where I wanted to be, albeit two years early. The road had not necessarily been a linear A to B, but through the twists and turns of the past six months I was on the doorstep of my mid-term goals. I could become an interim worker with a part-time role in a firm I loved for a boss I massively admired. Given the part-time nature of that role, I had more time with my family, as well as time to devote to WeAreTheCity and my other various charity and mentoring commitments.

There was no gold star above my door in terms of job title or the financial trimmings that came with my COO role anymore, but I was a step closer to achieving my longer term goals and contentment in my very own Emerald City.

THE EMERALD CITY

It was June 2010 and I was sitting in the beautiful Dorchester Hotel, the atmosphere could only be described as buzzing. There were hundreds of women and men around me, caught up in the excitement of the 2011 Women in Banking and Finance Awards. For the second year running, I had made the final three for the Women's Champion category. As I looked around, taking in every moment of the occasion, I found myself in awe of the smiling faces on every table. Although I had been there before, it didn't feel any less special, and the best part was that I knew even more of the people in the room a year on through my ongoing networking journey.

There was another difference this year, and that was that my network had morphed from just being good contacts to actually becoming dear friends, mentors and confidants. Over the years, they had celebrated various milestones with me but also seen me at what was probably one of my lowest points only a few months before.

At that point I had been back in my old firm for a month. When I sat at my desk on my first day back, the emotion I felt was indescribable. I was home. I felt safe again. While I was putting on a happy face, my confidence had been massively dented by the experiences of my previous role and it was going to take me a while to pull myself fully back together. However, I had recovered from tough knocks before and I knew I had it in me to overcome another.

Back at the awards, I watched the chairwoman of Women in Banking and Finance, Sylvana Caloni, take to the stage to announce the winner of my category. I took a deep breath as I looked around me, attempting to smile at the anxious faces on my table. They were all staring at me, rooting for me with their eyes, hearts and minds. It was lovely to feed off their enthusiasm while I tried to contain my own.

As the chairwoman began to read the biography of the winner, I felt a bubble that started in the pit of my stomach make its way up to the apples of my cheeks and emerge as the biggest smile you have ever seen. The people on my table and the tables around me had already started cheering – it was me she was describing, reading aloud the bio that had started life as a blank piece of paper! My name, my journey, there it was. I was never good at winning things in my life, not even when I had bought a majority of the raffle tickets on a tombola, not even an egg and spoon race – but here I was with one of the most prestigious awards on the networking circuit for a cause that was now embedded in the very heart of who I had become.

The riotous applause and "whoop whoops" that echoed from my friends at nearly every table in the grand hall of The Dorchester filled me with probably the most joy I have ever felt in my entire life. The look of pride on my mum's and dad's faces was something that will remain with me forever, I can still see it now. There was a knowing wink from my first-ever boss Roy whom I had invited to join me at the awards. He shouted above the noise of the audience: "The girl's done good!"

I picked up my award from Chris Sullivan, CEO of UK Corporate Banking at RBS. I held the glass object in my hands and what was probably a brief moment in time to the audience felt like an hour to me. Within that hour was a lifetime of flashbacks – tower blocks, bullying, fear, the City, Stewart, kids, smiles of joy, contentment in pockets, anxiety, tears of despair and now this. If ever the universe wanted to make its point about where I needed to be in life and what I needed to be doing, this was it.

Less than a month later, I met an amazing lady called Maggie Semple through a fellow networking contact, Amanda Phillips. Maggie was an ex non-executive director at the British Library and McDonald's as well as a sought-after coach for a number of senior leaders across the City. She was and still is a legend in her own right. I met her for coffee in the gorgeous Royal Exchange, right in the heart of my beloved City. After a meeting of spirits and minds where I offered to help her in her latest venture, she asked me what she could do for me by way of return. I rarely have an ask but if I do, it tends to be for others, but this time around I told her that my next goal was to obtain a non-executive director or trustee position within a charity, and should I be lucky enough to do so, I asked her to consider being my mentor. That played to my point that if you don't ask, you don't get, so you might as well ask big! Maggie's response was above and beyond what I had asked for. Not only did she offer to mentor me, but she also asked me to join the board for a charity called the National Youth Music Theatre. The charity was small enough for me to cut my teeth on and provide me with the experience I needed should I wish to pursue a bigger board position, but it was also an organisation for which I knew I could add value.

I dug out my bio and amended it once more. Vanessa Vallely, 22 years with senior level experience in IT, finance and banking, educated at Chicago Booth University, Financial News 100 Rising Star, WIBF Women's Champion, and non-executive director at the NYMT. I liked the look of that list much better than what I'd aspired to become between the ages of 15 and 35.

A few months later I was approached by a headhunter for a non-executive director position at a larger charity, Prostate Cancer UK. The board was looking to add several new trustee positions, and after seeing my CV and previous experience they wanted to meet me. I went through the interview process more for experience than anything else, as I really didn't expect to land a trustee role for what was a £20m charity, a medium-sized business in wider terms. I interviewed with some of the most amazing gentlemen I had ever met who were ex-chairmen, clinicians and surgeons to name but a few. During the interview they asked me what I thought I brought to the table. I mentioned my 22-year background in various senior positions and my expertise around execution, but the biggest thing I believed that I brought to the table for this organisation was my network and the ability to use my WeAreTheCity platform to help educate thousands of women about this cancer. It was a penny-dropping moment to realise that the value of my WeAreTheCity network extended far beyond advertising revenue and could help save people's lives. I realised that if women knew the early symptoms of prostate cancer and were educated about a disease that kills as many men as breast cancer does women, they will be the ones who nag their men to go to their GPs and get checked out.

I would also bring gender balance to their board. It was no surprise to hear at my interview that there were 10 men and only one other woman involved. Not much different from the FTSE boards then!

I was offered the position and didn't hesitate to accept it. I was infinitely more focused on thinking through what I could do to help shape the charity strategically and contribute to their ambitious growth plans. It was an opportunity to give back – notably this time to men – plus a chance to learn from a number of other amazing individuals with a much more diverse range of expertise than I had ever dealt with before.

With every month that passed, my confidence returned. The potholes of the past started to disappear and I felt like the future was mine again. And this time, when I got the second trustee role, my first move was not to reach for my bio to add it to my list to bolster my confidence. I knew what I was good at, I knew what I was capable of, and the titles on that piece of paper were no longer the litmus test for whether I was doing well. I was doing better than I ever expected I would, and finally, finally I was able to just get on with it.

The number of speaking events I was being asked to speak at was increasing outside of work, and after talking to endless numbers of women and men at these events I realised that many of them were still facing exactly the same issues I had been through earlier on in my career. I began to open up a little more about some of my more personal experiences, sharing tips on how I had overcome the hurdles I faced while building my career and attempting to manage relationships and a balanced home life. I didn't think it was my job to preach about how to deal with situations, but merely to share my own experiences; if hearing those experiences gave people ideas of their own, it would also reassure them that they were not alone in their various challenges. Where appropriate, I pointed them towards a variety of networks that had helped me. I was also suggesting mentors to guide them and sources of other support groups who would navigate them through a variety of storms. The number of emails I receive after my speaking events really makes me realise how many corporate individuals of all ages suffer in silence, be it career woes, the struggles to achieve balance, and the guilt of wanting things for themselves but giving their all to their children and partners and companies instead. Unfortunately, many of them have said they felt they had no support or anyone to turn to.

In terms of my day job, I was firing on all cylinders, taking on additional responsibility and delivering, albeit in a less aggressive and alpha manner. Through my experience I had come to recognise that it is not always the hare that wins the race and, as I said to my teams early in my career, small indications of progress should still be celebrated as progress, no matter how small.

Summer finally arrived in 2011. There is nothing quite like summer in the City of London, it's like the world of finance almost holds its breath for a few months and everyone is happier. On this particular day, the sun was shining and I was beaming having just returned from being a guest on BBC Woman's Hour, another one of my dreams that came to life through my long-term supporter and friend, Suzanne Doyle Morris.

Eating my sandwich with one hand and typing with the other, I received a phone call from a lady at EFinancial News asking me to attend a photo shoot for the EFinancial News FN100 awards. I didn't question why, I just checked the date to see if I could make it and agreed to attend, but I was slightly confused. I had been on their Rising Stars list the year before and wondered why they would be doing a photo shoot so much later. Never one to turn down the rare opportunity to be a bit pampered, I attended the photo shoot still slightly curious and a bit embarrassed to ask why I was there. As I went up the stairs and into the studio, there were a number of very high-profile women who I recognised from some of the big banks, but I didn't recall any of them being on the Rising Stars list the year before.

It wasn't long before I realised that the reason I was invited to attend the shoot was that I had made it on to a new list as one of the Top 100 Women in Finance across EMEA and Africa. I am still not sure to this day who nominated me that year, but whoever it was or however I got there, this is my opportunity to say thank you!

Towards the end of the year I was invited to Washington to pick up my first global award from The International Alliance for Women. I was nominated by the author of *Your Loss – How to Win Back Your Female Talent* and founder of diversity think tank Bidiversity, Christina Ioannidis. Christina had been a long-term supporter of mine and an individual who was key to my own networking journey. She was one of the first speakers I plucked up courage to approach at one of my first networking events before I had even set up WeAreTheCity. The award itself was to recognise and celebrate the top 100 women in the world who were making a notable difference to the economic empowerment of women. I remember receiving the email stating I had made the list; I just sat there in total shock. When I looked at the previous winners, there were all of my role models – amazing women who operated in the City including India Gary-Martin from JP Morgan, Helena Morrissey from Newton Investments, and Pinky Lilian who ran a number of major awards for women in the UK.

The best thing about going to Washington to pick up my award was that it allowed me to create another layer to my network, which this time was global. I worked with women throughout the conference who were from the Congo, India and the Middle East, and it was a really humbling experience to hear what some of them had done versus my challenges in the corporate world – it did put things into perspective for me.

For years I had wanted to travel to Africa after hearing stories from my brother and sister-in-law who had worked for many non-governmental organisations (NGOs) across Africa. Spending time with the women in Washington had just re-ignited my desire to do so, and a month later I was on my way. My plan was not to travel alone, but to convince some of my mentees to accompany me.

I wanted to offer my mentees much more than my experience, my contacts or my ability to open doors for them when they were not in the room. I wanted to push their boundaries and to give them a cultural experience of a lifetime. For a number of years, WeAreTheCity had supported a small orphanage called Forever Angels in Mwansa, just outside of Tanzania. Every year we would sponsor children or procure much-needed items to show our support; however I had long shared my deep desire to visit with the founder of the baby home, Amy Hathaway. Amy is a selfless and amazing individual who has devoted much of her own life to caring for orphaned children. Amy had turned her own dream into one of the biggest rehoming centres for children in that part of the continent. If you think we as corporate women or entrepreneurs face challenges, you need to spend a day in Amy's shoes to give yourself a sense of perspective.

I wanted to help her in some way while giving back to the women and children in that community. When Stewart asked me what I wanted by way of a gift for my 39th birthday, I said I wanted a plane ticket to Africa.

Many individuals, including me, harbour dreams; however, without actions they are exactly that, just dreams. Once my ticket was booked, I rounded up mentees to accompany me and raise funds for a myriad of small projects I wanted to execute on the visit. I wanted to take my mentees out of their normal operating environments and work with them in an environment where their creature comforts were stripped away. It wasn't long before three of them signed up to come with me which was followed by a fourth mentee I hadn't expected.

As I sat at home one evening, my 10-year-old was pushing her food around her plate, and like most youngsters in the UK she had no concept of food waste. I casually asked her if she knew how many children her wasted food would feed in a third world country. In a cheeky manner she said: "Why don't you let me come to Africa with you, then I can see for myself?" She proceeded to try and convince me that she could teach pre-school and look after the children at the orphanage. I didn't need convincing, I knew she could probably do it and I also knew what a life-altering experience it would be for her too. I decided to call her bluff, and I took my laptop out my bag and booked her flight there and then. I don't think she closed her mouth for two weeks. What probably started out in her mind as an opportunity to test her skills of parental persuasion had resulted in a trip to the other side of the world, eight injections and a course of malaria tablets.

I remember telling a number of my friends and colleagues that my 10-year-old daughter would be accompanying me and my mentees to Africa, and they questioned my sanity. Even Stewart took a bit of convincing. My view was that I had been lucky enough to grow up in a multicultural environment which I truly believe gave me a great understanding of how different people from different backgrounds can not only work together, but potentially build a better world. Why would I not want my child to have that experience? She lived in middle class Britain outside of London in one of the leafy suburbs. I didn't want either of my children to grow up thinking a) the world is white and b) that it is flat. There is an amazing world out there and if I could open the eyes of my children, my mentees and anyone else who was willing to come along for the ride, then why wouldn't I do that?

I took a week's leave from work and led my volunteer party out to Mwansa. Between us we raised over £7,500. Our intention was to not only visit, but to leave a legacy behind. We visited schools for the deaf and worked within the orphanage with children affected by HIV, cerebral palsy and hydrocephalus. We funded a refurbishment of a boys' refuge centre and left a donation in place to support a small micro finance operation which the parents of children of the home could benefit from. Just £50 would enable a young mum to set up her own business selling coal by the roadside, enough to enable her to generate her own income and take her children back into her own care.

I watched my mentees and my own daughter grow over that week in so many ways. We shared experiences and faced a few scary challenges that took us all out of our comfort zones; however, we travelled back to the UK realising just how lucky we were as individuals and with a feeling that we had made a difference in the world, no matter how small.

I am often asked how changing the lives of just one or two people warrants the effort. My theory has been that if just one of us touches the lives of another one or two, and we all engage in such activities, imagine how many lives we can touch as a collective. We should never assume that we don't have to contribute because other people are already contributing. I am a true believer that small endeavours by many can make big changes in the world.

My daughter changed dramatically after that trip. She came back much more appreciative of what she had in life and with a much better understanding of how important it is to help others. I was so glad I had called her bluff! I am sure she will end up working in an NGO or with a charity later in life having had that experience so young.

I vowed at that point that every year going forward I would travel, either alone or with my mentees, to work with women and children in different parts of the world to try and give back to society in terms of my time and experience, not just money.

As 2012 dawned, I was determined to continue the year in the same vein as 2011. I was asked to be involved in the London Olympics as part of my charity involvement with my alternative royal heritage, the Pearly Kings and Queens! Walking around the stadium at the opening ceremony in the company of the descendent of the original suffragette, Emmeline Pankhurst, and beside the legendary Chelsea pensioners and those amazing individuals who were re-enacting the arrival of Caribbeans on the Windrush, was a huge honour of another unforgettable sort entirely. I loved having the opportunity to wear my pearly suit that represented over 100 years of London's history.

By this point, I was already hankering for my next trip abroad to work with women elsewhere. I had been invited to speak to a group of women as part of Qatar's Women Leading Change programme. Their aim was to build a network and impart skills to facilitate their target of 20% females in senior corporate positions by 2015. Women Leading Change is an organisation spearheaded by yet another amazing woman I had met on the networking circuit called Rachel Petrero. As part of my endeavours to inspire women all over the world, I travelled to Qatar to spend three days broadening my understanding of the various challenges Qatari women face around building their businesses.

Before I took the stage at their conference, I wondered if my own career story would translate from a cultural perspective; after all, here I was citing a limited education while speaking to some of the most well-educated women in the world. My story of having no money wasn't something I was sure they would connect with, being one of the world's richest nations, but somehow they did.

I had had the same feeling when I had spoken in India on International Women's Day a couple of years earlier. The opportunity to speak was a pure fluke that came to pass as I was in Delhi on business. Despite our different backgrounds and cultures, we all seem to share the same fears, the same challenges, and in lots of ways we were all victims of various political and class systems. In India it was interesting to note that my story seemed to strike a chord not just with the women, but with the men too.

It was October 2012 and I had just returned from my travels to launch WeAreTheCity's new job board initiative, Careers City. Careers City was an idea generated by WeAreTheCity' members in response to a survey a year before where we asked them what more we could do on our site to support their careers. Thanks to four years of effort, our members now knew where to network and pick up more skills outside their corporate environments. They had benefited from the advice of over 250 female writers, they knew where to look for their mentors and now they wanted to expand their careers at firms that were proactively seeking to increase the numbers of women in their workforce. They wanted to go to companies who wanted them – it made absolute sense. Careers City was created for them. It was aimed at helping to build the pipeline and to raise awareness of the myriad career opportunities available to women across the UK, we also wanted to encourage women to return to the workplace after maternity leave by showing them that there were firms who were actively promoting flexible options.

We launched to an audience of over 100 prominent City recruiters and showcased speakers from over five generations of women, from age 60 to the youngest who was just 11 years old. She shared her views of our current world of work: she told us we all looked the same, spent way too much time on our phones and she reminded us all that it would only be 10 years until her generation was entering the City and would be snapping at our heels. She also shared her vision for the future. She told us that she expected to work in a world where colour, race and gender weren't an issue. She wanted to be able to wear what she liked and work from anywhere in world. She wanted to be hired for the skills she had, and her ability to do a job and do it well. It will come as no great surprise when I tell you that that apple had not fallen far from the tree – the 11-year-old was my daughter.

The year ended as it began. I was turning 40 and alongside all of my other commitments as a corporate worker, mum, charity trustee and website owner, I had also managed to complete a bucket list of 40 things I wanted to do before I turned 40. From things as simple as childhood visits that I never had to running the London Marathon, I managed to cram it all into just under nine months.

By now, I had spoken to over 5,000 women and 2,000 men across 60 organisations, sharing advice and tips on how they could grow their careers. I had raised over £25,000 for charity in that year alone and travelled across continents in my bid to share stories and help women of different cultures. It was a good thing I never took much notice of all the individuals along the way who told me what I couldn't do or would never become.

I put everything I have ever achieved down to hard work and the support of a few very special people. I also attribute it to my passion and spirit as no matter how many times I was put down or let down, I just came back fighting. I don't believe in the words 'it can't be done' or 'I will never achieve', because you can and you will, you just have to want whatever you desire badly enough to work for it. I wanted to write this book, not just because it was number 40 on my bucket list, but because I wanted to share what I had learned about corporate life and how I survived and thrived against all odds. You may well read some of the tips that follow and nod in agreement as they appear to be common sense, however, back to my question at the start of the book, are you practising them or using these methods to accelerate or position your own career? If you read on and find that you know most of these tips already then great stuff, please pass the book on to someone else who may be in need of a few ideas to boost their careers. If you read on and find that there are things you could put into practice, then even better – the book has been worthwhile writing.

So now it's all about you and how you can expedite your success. In terms of what I did next – well, you will just have to wait until the end of the book to find out.

TIPS FOR YOUR CAREER SUCCESS

ACHIEVING CAREER SUCCESS IN THE CORPORATE JUNGLE

"Don't just survive it, thrive in it" – *Vanessa Vallely*

There is no one right way to survive corporate life, and success is not only defined differently by everyone, it's achieved differently by everyone too. What follows is a framework full of ideas that you can use to propel your own careers.

Despite eventually achieving my goal to reach a senior position in the City, I didn't always make good decisions, especially when it came to people. The bad decisions have provided as much learning as the decisions that brought me success and there is equal value in both. Please take my stories and tips to provoke your own thoughts as you refine your own career plans and route to success.

There are 13 key areas that I wish to focus on throughout the rest of this book. I believe if you read and take elements of each one, you will accelerate your career or business in some guise.

Everything in life for me starts with a plan, so let's start there. As the quote by Benjamin Franklin states, failure to plan is planning to fail!

CREATING YOUR CAREER PLAN - MISSION AND STRATEGY

"What can't be measured doesn't get done" – Peter Drucker

Don't underestimate the importance of having a plan. For the past 10 years I have set out intentions for my overall career ambition, my strategy and my goals on paper to ensure that I am clear about what I need to do and can refer back to what I've agreed with myself.

By adopting this method and staying true to what I have said to myself that I was going to do, I believe that I moved considerably faster through my career than I would have if I had just waited for fate to play its hand. Planning provides you with an operating structure and helps you measure your progress. By having a plan, it can keep you focused and in times of doubt you will also have something to remind yourself about what you have set out to achieve.

The time you spend creating your plan should be seen an investment in yourself. Plans on paper are physical tools that will enable you to keep yourself on track, but the ethos of your plan is in everything you do and the time you put into certain activities. When you sit down to create your plan, it will make you think about your bigger picture and it may take some time. There is a lot to be said about taking time out to think!

You don't necessarily have to have a career strategy when you start out, it could be something you focus on midway through working life when the time is right or something you adopt after reading this book. It was only when I discovered the importance of having a wider plan and the methods to support it that I stopped slipping off the rungs of the ladder and actually started to climb it!

Having a personal mission statement

Everyone has a purpose, be it in their career or in life. A good way of helping to recognise your purpose and focus your efforts on your career is to create a personal mission statement. Your personal mission statement is a clear articulation of where you are going and what your purpose is. Your mission is then supported by your strategy and finally a list of goals. Think of it like this:

- Your mission – what you aim to achieve in the long term

- Your strategy – how you are going to get there

- Your goals – what you need to do to achieve your strategy and overall mission

The experts will advise you to make your mission statement measurable and to feature some form of timeline. While I agree in principle, I actually see the measurable aspect of my mission statement contained at a more granular level within my goals, as each of those have a date attached to them in some form.

To bring this to life, here is an example of a very early mission statement I wrote when I first started work.

To save enough money (THE WHAT) to move mum and me away from our environment in London (THE WHY) within three years (THE WHEN).

In order to achieve my mission, I needed to have a strategy. Your strategy is how you will achieve your mission.

Below is an example of my strategy which explains how I am going to do it and by when:

To secure a professional role in a bank at a salary of at least £7,500 (THE HOW) and save £2,000 towards a house deposit over three years (THE WHEN).

Adding the 'when' into all your statements regardless of whether it's your mission, strategy or even goals you set downstream is the most important part of the process. Setting dates for things to be completed drives progress and ultimately gives you something to work towards. Back to the quote at the opening of the chapter, you want to make sure you are getting things done.

After I've articulated my mission and my strategy, I would then have various goals that I needed to achieve in order to achieve the overall plan.

Below is an example of my goals which detail what I need to do in order to achieve my strategy:

- **Secure a job in a bank within the salary range specified within six months (THE WHAT and TIMEFRAME)**

- **Save £2,000 within three years (THE WHAT and TIMEFRAME).**

There would then be a number of lower level tasks in order to achieve the above, for example:

1. **Research jobs**

2. **Apply for jobs**

3. **Investigate savings account options**

4. **Open savings account**

So now let's look at my example plan in its final form.

Mission

To save enough money to move mum and me away from our environment in London within three years.

My Strategy

To secure a professional role in a bank at a salary of at least £7,500 and save £2,000 towards a house deposit over three years.

My Goals

To secure a job in a bank within the salary range specified within three months.

Save £2,000 within three years.

Tasks

Research jobs
Apply for jobs
Investigate savings account options
Open savings account

The key here is that when you write your goals, they should be supporting activities that refer to your strategy in some way. If you are finding that a number of them don't, then you need to consider why you are investing time in them at all! If your goals are not supporting where you want to go in the long term, then you won't be taking the steps towards your overall mission.

That said, life is not all about work. There are occasions when there is something you may want to do that isn't necessarily aligned to your strategy or your overall mission – in which case, do it, but ensure you weigh up the time you spend on these goals as opposed to the ones that are going to progress your career. It's your timeline after all!

SETTING YOURSELF GOALS

Without goals, there are no aims; without aims, there is no aspiration; and without aspiration there is no achievement – the strategy doesn't pan out and the mission doesn't get achieved, it's as simple as that.

I have been setting myself goals from as far back as I can remember, and in some instances they've even helped me achieve far above what I originally set out to do.

Earlier on in my career I didn't realise that I needed a strategy or a mission, and I effectively wasted a fair bit of time. What started out as two or three goals per year when I was younger has turned into as many as 40 later on in life. Practice makes perfect! Goals do not always have to be large life-changing events, they can be small things that either satisfy your current aspirations or contribute towards your overall life and career strategy.

Every year around New Year I sit down with my family and we talk about our goals for the year. Not New Year resolutions, but goals. Such is my love of goals, we use this mechanism to achieve things together as a family too. It's actually been a brilliant way to ensure that we are communicating and we all understand why we're individually doing what we're doing on a daily basis or why we're behaving a certain way – when we all know what each person is working to, it also makes it a lot easier to support each other.

At the start of the year and generally over a family dinner, my husband and the children will speak about their individual goals for the year ahead, and then we discuss and agree our collective goals as a family. Above all, we all agree to help and support each other to achieve our goals. Most families probably do this in some guise; however, we have to take a slightly more structured approach to it because we are a working family with two businesses and a number of other commitments, and if we don't put stakes in the ground, things slip. For example, writing this book was one of my goals that I discussed with both my husband and the children as we went into 2013. I knew it would take my time away from them periodically over a period of three to four months, and I needed their buy-in in order for me to be able to get it done. I also needed to ensure that this wouldn't put pressure on my husband in any way, as he had his own things going on over the same time period. Together we discussed the book goal and how it would enable me to contribute to our mission as a family, and everyone agreed to support it – and true to their word, they have.

It's not just the grown-ups setting our goals, the children have their goals as well. Their goals have often been as simple as one of them wanting to learn how to swim. Their goals get included in the family plans. My husband and I review our wider strategy and check back that our now joint mission remains achievable and relevant for the years ahead.

When it comes to goal setting, I tend to split my goals into five key categories:

1. Life

2. Financial

3. Work

4. Personal

5. Home

My children have added another category here called Fun which is always full of wonderful things we pledge to do as a family. Everyone has to have at least one fun goal otherwise life becomes nothing but a list of serious to do's, and life is way too short for that! So, for the kid in all of us, here is no.6

Fun

Life goals tend to appear again and again, often over multiple years. An example of a life goal if we look back over the later stages of my career would be that I want to give up working in the corporate world by the time I am 45. Life goals tend to be the grand goals, whereas the goals in the other categories tend to be their enablers.

Financial goals could be something like clearing my credit cards, reducing my outgoings by 10% or even something as simple as changing my mortgage provider to secure a better deal. Negotiating a pay rise could also fall into this category (or the work category).

Work goals could be related to something that you want to learn, a promotion you aspire to or a particular skill you wish to hone, eg. public speaking or confidence in meetings. Remember these are not the same goals that you may have detailed as part of your corporate work objectives, these could be completely separate and play more to your longer term career plan.

Personal goals are exactly that – they are personal to you for whatever reason. These could be learning a new skill like making sushi, spending more time with your family or even to do with your health, eg giving up smoking, doing a five-kilometre run, cycling to work and so on.

Home goals for me tend to be more of a task-orientated list. These could be about a room I need to decorate or larger maintenance jobs that may need doing. Sometimes these have included more big-ticket goals like moving house or planning an extension for my office. There have even been times when one of my home goals was to actually spend more time at home!

The fun goal tends to be ticking a box around something I have always wanted to do that is not work or home related. I had 40 fun goals the year I celebrated my 40th birthday, which meant some of the others had to take a bit of a back seat. My fun goals included everything from attending Royal Ascot to recording a CD with my best friends and throwing a party with a Willy Wonka theme.

Once I have set my goals (the 'what'), I then also look at the 'who and what else', as in who or what else I might need to help me to achieve my goals. It may not necessarily be people; it may be other things such as money, time, learning and so on. Once I have worked out what it is I need, I detail those things or individuals next to each goal. I then create another column where I map out the 'how', which looks at what I need to do at a more granular level in order to move towards my goals.

My last step is to set a timeline for my goals. I tend to use quarters in line with how the business world tends to view time (Q1 is January-March, Q2 is April-June etc.), as it is a little more flexible than placing additional pressure on myself to reach an exact date. There are occasions when your goals will have a hard stop date due to the nature of the goal, and if that's the case, you need to add the date in. This could be something like needing to redo a room by 10th June when other family members are coming over to stay. I often find that once my draft goal plan is finished and I can see all my goals on an A3 sheet, I actually need to reorder or reprioritise them, as there may well be dependencies between them or a certain sequence that would make them easier to execute.

My goals plan is also my success tracker. I review it in detail every three months. I tend to perform a shorter review on a monthly basis as things and priorities may have changed. At mid-year I also review my goals and ask myself whether I am on track. Have I put in enough effort to achieve my goals? Are there other people I've met since I started my planning who might be able to help me? If you imagine a corporate mid-year review, this is no different, except you happen to be both the reviewer and the one executing the goals. You need to be totally honest with yourself when self-reviewing. It is really easy to make 101 excuses as to why you couldn't fit something in or why something didn't get done. I can only tell you what my nan used to say in circumstances like this: it's your boat, and it's up to you whether you swim out to it or watch it from the harbour!

Here's the call to action if you want to try this form of planning for yourself. Take yourself away from work and home once you've finished this book to pen your own mission statement. Go somewhere where you are outside of your normal environment, and free from interruptions – an hour should be sufficient time so your local coffee bar is probably a good place to start. You are not meant to be writing chapter and verse, but the plan should detail what you wish to achieve over the next few years. Some people prefer to write it in bullet point form or you can also write it like a story in the third person, especially if you feel quite far away from where you want to go. Whatever way you write it, it must be at a very high level (no low-level detail, that comes later). That's your first step done.

Over the next week you can start to write down your overall strategy around how you think you are going to achieve your mission. You may find you play with this part of the process for a period of time and you should let yourself have enough time to daydream a bit about various options and get a few ideas before you put pen to paper.

Once that's done, you'll want to start the more granular process of setting the goals that sit under your strategy, using the method of categorisation mentioned earlier if this works for you, and remember to include the later stages of your planning by including who, how and when.

You should view your plan as a living document, not something you take out annually to dust off and update. You can be working with it all of the time. Your mission statement, on the basis that it doesn't change, should remain fairly static; however, your strategy and underlying goals may need to flex here and there as situations and priorities change.

Most importantly, you don't need to wait until the New Year to start! You could start today and run your year from September to September, or April to April. It really makes no difference just as long as you make a start.

I also find sharing my plan and goals with others helps, especially when they are people who may be able to help me achieve my goals. Bear in mind you may not always need just one person. Sometimes you might need whole groups of people, and this is where the networking side of things comes into play. The more people you know, the more people there will be to help you.

When you achieve one of your goals, remember to celebrate. Pat yourself on the back in whatever form that takes. Think about what you would do if you were the leader of a team and one of your employees did something that was just amazing – you would reward them, right? So why not reward yourself? If you don't, you will soon get bored with constantly pushing on, trying to achieve all the time.

Managing your career and your life is a bit like a business, and because there are similarities it is helpful to mirror some of the same processes a business would have. Businesses follow a structure to ensure they grow and progress, and you need to think of yourself in the same context. Live and breathe your mission, review your strategy regularly, plan your goals, reward yourself when you achieve something, and don't forget to include that little bit of fun along the way!

LEARN EVERY DAY

"A day spent without learning something is a day wasted" –Anonymous

I have spent most of my career learning in one way or another. For me, life and your career should be one continuous cycle of discovering new things and self-improvement. In the early days of my career I was always reading books, but learning resources now come in a wide variety of easily accessible formats, eg. webinars, mentors, networking events as well as conventional books and training courses, so you can choose the format that works best for you.

Whatever job you take on most likely involves some form of learning in order to perform the role. I have always chosen to over-learn (if there is such a thing) in order to perform the role to the best of my ability. By this I mean that I don't just learn above and beyond in terms of my direct role, but I invest time in understanding many of the other roles around the periphery of my job. This allows me to not only build key relationships but to also gain a deeper understanding of the end-to-end processes of others. Showing interest in the bigger picture and not just within your own part of the working world reaps rewards, but it will take time and effort on your part.

Just to show you what this means in practical terms, in my role as a business manager I may need to create a report for my COO. I could ask whoever is responsible for providing me with the data to send it over and I would create the report, give it to my boss and the job is done. Alternatively, the learning approach would be to ask the individual to show me how they gather the data for the report, find out where it comes from, create the report, look it over and go back and ask the person who gave me the data the questions that I think the boss might ask, before handing it over. Doing the latter has enabled me to engage with others, learn about a new process and add value to my boss. In that scenario, what's happened in the past is that I've already uncovered problems before the report went to my boss and I was able to resolve them so they never had a chance to become his problem, and he got a clean report – your average boss is not going to argue with that!

In terms of continuing to learn, there have been times when I have taken on a new role knowing that I cannot do 100% of what is on the job description. There was a recent study by Europe's Institute of Leadership and Management which showed that 20% of men will apply for a role despite only partially meeting its job description, compared to 14% of women, take note all female readers, you need to be conscious of what you're up against and push your boundaries a little more as it appears more guys are willing to learn on the job than women! When I do take on a new role and I know I have knowledge gaps, I ensure that during the first few months in my role I add a learning plan to my career toolkit (your toolkit will be explained later on in the book). This may be via online learning, attending an industry event, leveraging the experience of colleagues or mentors or by reaching out to someone in my network asking them to share their expertise in an area where my own knowledge is limited.

Whenever I join a new firm or department, I ensure my first couple of weeks are spent meeting and learning about all of my key stakeholders, their roles and their challenges. Once I have met them, I then request time with their teams to deepen my understanding of their function and key processes – again, this method leads to learning and relationship building opportunities.

I use mentors and coaches where necessary and often make full use of the experienced individuals around me by asking them to teach me things where my understanding is lacking or needs refreshing. Again, asking tends not to be a natural trait for women and in truth many people generally feel uncomfortable about asking for help because they think it may make them look less competent.

On a number of occasions I have approached key individuals and asked them if they would allow me to sit in their meetings in order to listen and learn about their field or projects. I always let them know that I don't want to join in the meeting, I merely want to observe in the background in order to gain a better understanding of the subject. More often than not, when I have used this method of on-the-job learning, I have not even been part of the team or division involved in the meeting. However, I felt that if I attended a few of their meetings this would allow me to learn about their particular project or initiative. I would often sell this learning activity to my line managers as a development opportunity and ask them if it would be OK to attend at least two of these external meetings a month. They rarely said no, and a number of them said they were impressed I was taking the initiative. More often than not, people try to get out of going to meetings rather than attending them, so I was usually welcomed with open arms by the people holding the meetings I wanted to go to!

I used this method to gain an understanding of a number of subjects throughout my career, and as a consequence I learned about new subjects that weren't relevant to my role at the time, but turned out to be crucial later on. You may want to consider writing yourself a list of things that you wish to learn about more generally, and then think about who in your network would be able to teach you or introduce you to someone who could help.

To give you an example, there was a large derivatives programme being run at one of the firms I worked for. The subject of derivatives was of significant interest to me even though derivatives trading had nothing to do with my current position in IT. I approached the programme manager and explained that I was keen to learn. I asked him to share the programme brief and asked him whether he would consider letting me sit in on a couple of project briefings and perhaps spend time with one of his business analysts. He agreed. I then returned to my boss with the proposition, stating that the programme manager had agreed to let me sit and observe as long as it was OK with my boss. My boss also agreed as he saw this as development time that he didn't have to pay for and keenness on my part to learn new things.

It is this sort of proactive behaviour that also gets you noticed and helps you to build relationships across your firm. In this particular instance, after a few months of attending the derivatives meetings I had gained a very basic understanding of the concept. I probably still couldn't trade a derivative, however I understood the terminology and complexity and enough about the systems and processes in order to have a basic conversation – all of which fuelled additional questions and helped to deepen my understanding of the subject. More importantly, it built my confidence in talking about the topic in an organisation where derivatives were an important part of our business.

Another way I learn is by observing people and their leadership styles. I have been lucky enough to be on more than eight senior leadership teams throughout my career, and if I am totally honest these have probably been the biggest learning grounds of my career. Observing other leaders and how they deal with situations is fascinating, and if you're paying attention it's usually quite obvious to see what works and what doesn't. I have often taken these lessons and supplemented them with my own views and opinions of how I would have handled a similar situation. Styles of others should not necessarily always be emulated, and being your authentic self is paramount, especially as you get higher up the ladder.

In order to keep your learning up to date around innovation within your sector, I believe that joining a membership body for your particular profession is a huge step towards not only learning new things, but keeping yourself up to date with industry standards, best practice and any burning issues. You can benefit not only from the events run by these organisations, but you can also build a solid peer and networking group in your sector (all of which you should connect to via some form of social media). This peer group is invaluable, not just for future roles but for future advice and leveraging experiences too.

There are so many events that you can capitalise on if you want to learn outside of work from the thousands of networks that exist in London alone, let alone across the UK and further afield. One of the main reasons we created an events calendar on WeAreTheCity was to promote these various learning opportunities in one centralised place so members of our site could learn and grow. Of course, there are universities and many other adult education providers running events and courses too, so there is a lot to choose from out there!

No matter how much information an event can provide, ultimately it's you that needs to a) appreciate the importance of continuous learning in terms of your career and b) take the initiative and find time to invest in yourself. Even if it's only two hours a week, that still translates to a day a month, and it's the least you can give yourself if you are really serious about your career.

I also have a learning plan. I still designate eight hours per month to learn something new or to supplement my knowledge in an area that I am either just generally interested in or have a particular need to get better at. I also network at least once a week and try to acquire a new skill every month. Sometimes these learning opportunities come naturally through my work, but other times I have to orchestrate the opportunity. Think of yourself in the context of continuous improvement. No matter how well we may feel we know our profession or the tools or skills it takes to get the job done, there are always new technologies, new methods, frameworks and approaches and new people with new ideas coming into our industries, and it's good to stay at the forefront.

In summary, keep looking for opportunities to learn, show willingness within your environment to find out what the other parts of your business do (even if they are not your key stakeholders or departments you normally interact with), be proactive, invest the time in yourself, and the biggest lesson in this chapter is don't be afraid to ask for help.

BUILD STRONG RELATIONSHIPS

"A relationship is an investment that will build as you continue to devote your time and effort. The more you put in, the more you'll get back" – Sumesh Nair

Building relationships with others is probably the most fundamental ingredient to your career success. Do not underestimate the time and investment required in order to make these relationships work. The naive approach would be to just invest time with those in your immediate working vicinity, however you will reap far more rewards if you cast your net further afield. This is a very narrow approach and will not reap the same rewards as casting your net further. You need to build relationships up and down your organisation, and this includes all of the supporting functions too. The power of the PA, the post boy and the receptionists, right the way through to the security guards as you enter the building, should be approached with as much enthusiasm and interest as you show to your boss's peer group and other senior figures. Who you know will very much dictate the speed, quality, and innovative nature of how you can get things done.

The first step, both in terms of the job you are doing and your future career plan, is to identify your key stakeholders. Once you know who they are, you then need to prioritise them in terms of your required interactions or projects. The next step is to engage with them to understand their expectations, needs and interests, and from there you can begin to build your relationship. This is not a one-off engagement, and it's not an exercise you can go into with selfish intent. It's the beginning of an ongoing process where you invest time and effort in getting to know the individuals.

In any job I have held, I haven't just invested time with my key stakeholders, but I have also invested time in *their* key stakeholders too. By understanding the role they also play I get a better sense of the bigger picture. Some of my previous peers have suggested that I just have a natural skill and ability to influence key stakeholders, I have to disagree. This is not a natural ability at all. It is something I have worked hard at by spending time with my stakeholders, understanding their needs and delivering to their expectations. More importantly, I offer to help them long before I ask them to help me. I also communicate constantly with all of my stakeholders. It is most definitely not just about talking to people when times are bad or when I need something, but more often than not on occasions where nothing is required at all. Even if it's a quick email every fortnight, or dropping them a link to an article that may be of interest to them, I am ever present in terms of our relationship. I also ensure that if I commit to doing something for my stakeholders, I follow through in line with their expectations. If I am delayed in any way on delivering, I manage their expectations beforehand.

Success in terms of managing key stakeholders is all about listening, communicating, empathy and, ultimately, delivery. If you communicate regularly around both the good and the bad, listen to their needs and do what you say you're going to do for them, you will help drive strong relationships that can deliver for you when you need them to. Simple stuff, but so very effective.

This is not to say that you commit to delivering everything they want, but by building strength early on in your relationship, when things get tough you can rely on your previous track record of delivery and have an adult conversation about what can be done and what cannot. It really is about managing expectations in a timely and honest fashion.

The best piece of advice I can offer here is to never neglect any of these relationships, or if you find that some relationships are taking up more time than others, ensure you communicate why to all your other stakeholders. Think about how great it would be to have a reputation amongst your key stakeholders for being someone who always tries to beat expectations – what do you need to do to be that person?

As a practical tip, you could create yourself a stakeholder map. I recommend http://www.stakeholdermap.com/ to my mentees as a site that is full of detailed tips, tricks and templates for stakeholder mapping. Although this site is more aligned with the project process of stakeholder mapping, the general concept can be applied to a number of stakeholder engagements.

As an exercise, try mapping your key stakeholders at work from a day-to-day business as usual perspective (eg. your boss, his/her peers, relationships with other supporting functions), then add an additional set from a career progression perspective which may include people like your line manager, HR, your mentors, your coaches and others. Bear in mind you may well want to include organisations as opposed to individuals for this as well. You may find that you have gaps here so this is where you will need to go and invest time building these relationships. Don't forget that one of the most important stakeholder groups for your career is people you don't work with – like your partner, other family members and close friends. These are often the people whose expectations you need to manage particularly closely, especially in busy or pressured times.

It is fair to say that if you complete this exercise it may look somewhat daunting and you probably didn't realise that all of these people are integral to your career success. However, back to my planning point, by knowing who your key stakeholders are it will enable you to focus your time more effectively on the management of these relationships in order to make them successful.

FIND YOUR INNER VOICE - BE CONFIDENT

"No one can make you feel inferior without your consent"– Eleanor Roosevelt

Throughout the very early part of my career there were many times where I let my lack of confidence or the opinions of others get the better of me. I feared if I put my head above the parapet that someone would inevitably chop it off. I would often sit silent in meetings, scared to share my opinions or put forward my ideas, or speak of previous experience, even when I knew that I had the experience to comment and add value. I was afraid that someone would think I was stupid or, worse still, cut my ideas down in a public forum. There was more than one occasion as I sat tight-lipped, almost on the edge of my seat, the words were just about to pour from my mouth, when bam, someone else would say the very thing that I wanted to, or share the same ideas as I had. I could have kicked myself a thousand times over for not speaking up sooner.

Having the confidence to speak up, make a statement or ask that question comes with time, experience and practice.

One of my mentees approached me recently about this exact scenario. She knew she could add value to a series of meetings she was attending but her lack of confidence was getting the better of her. She had also just moved teams and wanted to make a good impression. Her previous boss had made an issue about her lack of input in meetings, which then exacerbated the issue in her own mind. She now felt that everyone thought she didn't know her stuff because she was so quiet.

During our mentoring session we spoke about the fact that is it OK if you are not always the first to the table when it comes to ideas. Some individuals like to sit back, listen and think. We discussed alternative ways that she could perhaps share her thoughts with her colleagues.

One of the ways I overcame my fear of putting forward my ideas in large group situations was by gaining buy-in from my peers or stakeholders prior to big meetings. I would book a one-to-one discussion with some of the people who I knew would be in the meeting I was concerned about, and I'd discuss my thoughts and gather theirs ahead of time. I would suggest that I planned to bring up a particular issue, not mentioning my lack of confidence around doing so, and could already get their feedback on what I planned to say so I could decide whether to go ahead or not. If they were on board, during the big meeting I would present my ideas and say that I had discussed this previously with X and Y before presenting my ideas. This approach didn't make me feel so alone in the room as there were then more people there who I knew were on-side.

This method is also something that you will use later on in your career as you become more senior; however, it is not so much for confidence but more to get the input and consensus of your stakeholders before you present your ideas. It is easier to have what might be difficult conversations and take the time to influence people before you are in an open forum. In doing so, you will know who has bought into your ideas or the issues they are likely to raise. This will also enable you to do your homework and explore every avenue possible before you go in to present your pitch.

I discussed this method with my mentee, knowing that if she learned how to do it now to build her confidence it would also be a great skill for the future. She tried it and it worked, and her next task was just to practise it and find her inner voice in future meetings.

The true test will come when she needs to present an idea that no one has bought into and convince individuals in an open forum to agree to it. You learn to develop a thicker skin when not all of your ideas will fly, and there will be occasions where individuals are difficult purely because they can be, or they have other personal agendas. My advice here is don't give up if you think your ideas have weight, I am a true believer that persistence pays off in the end. That said, you may need to consider the timing of your idea and the fact that there may well be political reasons why others are being obstructive, so it will be a judgement call on your part how far or how long to pursue your idea if you're not getting anyone behind you.

My biggest piece of advice here is to know your limitations in terms of where you have influence within your organisation, but also know your convictions. If it is an idea that you cannot get through normal channels or you are not in the right meetings to do so, then consider which one of your stakeholders has the power to take your ideas to the right table and stand some chance of making it happen. Sometimes if you don't ask someone else to help you, your idea may never see the light of day.

LEAD BY EXAMPLE

"A leader is one who knows the way, goes the way, and shows the way" — John Maxwell

There are many different styles of good and effective leadership, but for me it is about the behaviours you exhibit day in and day out. We all have the capacity to be leaders in some form and should act in that capacity regardless of our job titles or positions.

My personal opinion is that I don't believe leadership is something that can be taught entirely through training or coaching. I believe it's a combination of learning the theory, learning through others, real hands-on experience and by learning from your own mistakes that will ultimately make you a successful leader.

I also believe that every leader needs to experience good times and bad times in order to fully understand the scope of a leadership role. It can be relatively easy to lead in the good times, but when the chips are down or the pressure is on, a real leader will be tested and show their true potential.

Something to bear in mind that you will be faced with as a leader is that it's almost impossible to predict situations that may arise, or indeed manage the culture and people aspects that are so often the most challenging aspects to trying to lead a team or organisation successfully.

I am a true believer in authentic leadership and in leading by example. Be true to yourself, be honest, genuine, free of personal agenda, and transparent, and above all never ask someone to do something you wouldn't be prepared to do yourself. For me, it's about empathy. It's also about gaining trust with individuals and about doing the right thing, especially in difficult times.

The best leaders appreciate that different people bring different views, opinions, and ways of working and learning. Diversity of thought should be warmly welcomed to ensure you get healthy debate and a variety of ideas. It's not just about having an open door policy, but encouraging individuals to walk through it and share their true thoughts. It's about setting the bar and living your own values and ethics, and standing by the decisions you make. It is about surrounding yourself with the right individuals and supporting their progress and growth, ensuring they know what part they play in any journey.

It is about being a strong communicator, and helping to build the right culture, staying conscious that you have a team of people looking to you to lead them, no matter what challenges you may face. It is about celebrating together in success and supporting your team through failure, often standing ahead of them to catch the fallout. It's about consistency in your behaviour to your teams and peers, because your success will often be measured by the success of the teams you lead – it's no longer about just what you can do. It's about making tough decisions and often standing your ground when you feel you are the only one in the room who wants to head in a particular direction.

It's about providing air cover and support to allow innovation and creativity to flow from your teams. You may be respected but not necessarily loved. You need the ability to stay strong and composed through the wildest of storms. It's about showing support and welcoming the ideas of others, but at the end of the day you are in charge – you must steer the ship when consensus amongst others is failing and clear direction is required. Dwelling on past mistakes can be a danger when the future continues to rush towards you. It's about being fearless, but not about being scared to show you are human at the same time.

Leadership can be a lonely place plagued with pressure and great expectations from others, and it's not a role that everyone is prepared to take. There can, however, be amazing rewards from leading others towards success and watching from a distance as they soar under your guidance.

You don't have to be leading a company, a business or a large team to put some of these key behaviours in place. You can start to demonstrate these behaviours even before you start managing people – often it is the fact that you are already demonstrating some of the these qualities that will get you noticed in the first place for a role that includes people management responsibilities.

Growing within a leadership role will take time, effort and consideration. Your ability to see the wider picture and to envision the potential impact of your decisions is paramount. If you get your leadership style right, there is no place people won't follow you. If you get it wrong, regardless of how brilliant you might be at the technical parts of your role, you will be remembered for failing your people.

There are thousands of leadership books available, and countless courses and events that you could attend to shape your thinking around your own leadership style from an academic perspective. A good resource is The Institute of Leadership and Management (www.i-l-m.com/). My personal view is that nothing beats hands-on experience, so read the books and take the courses but also make sure you're finding places to practise what you've learned.

So, how do you get leadership skills on your CV if they are not part of your day job? You could seek opportunities to show your leadership capability either within work or outside – this could be something as simple as leading a charity initiative or running a small project. Employee networks are another great place to gain those skills if you can volunteer to be involved in working on a committee. Make sure your line managers are aware of your aspirations in this respect, and remember to add any leadership experience to your CV and LinkedIn profile so a wider audience can get to know about your experience too!

IMPRESS YOUR BOSS

"If you always do what you always did, you will always get what you always got"– Albert Einstein

There are many ways you can be effective in your role. One way to stand out from the crowd is to impress your boss by making them as effective as they can possibly be. I have spent the past 25 years working with and for some of the busiest CEOs and COOs in the City, and I learned that it makes a difference to put yourself in their shoes and try to think like them so you can anticipate their needs. It's a valuable learning experience to think about what they think about anyway, as one day you may very well be in the role currently held by your own boss. Always think big!

Be prepared

Always come to a meeting prepared. Be on time, look the part and have everything you need to conduct an efficient and timely meeting. If you are meeting external companies, always have your business cards handy (and if possible carry a couple for your manager too). Ensure you have your relevant papers (and an extra copy). If there are documents that you may need to refer to in meetings, ensure you have sufficient copies for everyone there who may also need to refer to them. About five minutes before the meeting, collect your boss on the way so you both have time to discuss the plan of action before the meeting. If the meeting is very important (eg. if you expect a lot of decisions to be made there) I would always suggest a pre-meeting the day before to prepare. If you are having a one-to-one with your boss, send them an agenda a day or so before. This doesn't have to be formal, it can be a few bullet points on an email. This will help them structure their thoughts before the meeting and make your time together more productive.

Always stick to time in your meetings with your boss; arrive on time and wrap the meeting up a few minutes before the end of your time slot. Your boss's time is precious so make sure they know you appreciate that by being timely and structured yourself.

Act as a confidant

Build trust with your boss and become their sounding board. Your boss should be able to tell you most things (without compromising confidentiality), safe in the knowledge that what is discussed will stay within your circle of trust. This is incredibly important – anything that you tell anyone else is in a position to be leaked, regardless of how well you think you know the person you are telling. The best policy is not to tell anyone any confidential information you have been given, full stop. Being known as someone who never contributes idle gossip will increase the trust between you and your boss, and you will be viewed as a more serious player in the organisation. On the other hand, being the eyes and ears on the ground for your boss will be greatly appreciated. Senior managers don't often know what is happening on the shop floor, so if you can provide an anecdotal organisational temperature check that can be a great help. This is not about ratting on specific colleagues. You can plant seeds in your boss's mind about where they might soon be facing issues if they don't act. For example, if staff are thinking of leaving because there is an issue that is not being addressed by senior management, you suggest to your boss that morale may need a boost in certain areas.

Always give an extra 20%

It feels great to be known as the person who goes the extra mile and gets the job done. People who go beyond what is expected of them not only learn more as a consequence, but they impress those around them. Don't just complete the task, but think around the task and look forward. What else needs doing as a result of you completing your task, and how could you make it easier for the next person? Can you create a process to make it simpler if the same situation arises again? Just because someone has not asked you to do something, it doesn't mean it doesn't need doing, and if you're in a position to sort something out before you're asked to do it, then go for it. Don't just throw a task that you feel you have completed over the fence – stay with it until the end and take ownership, especially if it is urgent. Many people run away from taking ownership of anything outside their day job responsibilities as it can be more difficult and provide a few more headaches, but at the same time it is a strong leadership trait to take responsibility and see things through. It's always frustrating to deal with people who say "that's not my job" and leave it at that. It's much better to hear "that's not my job, but leave it with me and I'll sort it out anyway." Which person do you want to be known as?

Think like the boss

If you are preparing a document for your boss and you have discussed what they need you to do, before you give it back to your boss put yourself in his/her shoes and look at the document. Does it tell the right story in a compelling and easy to understand way? Do you need to add something else to complete the picture or conversely, is the story so cluttered as to be confusing? If you are looking at data and are still left asking a question, no doubt someone else will too. You could always create a copy and add what you believe the document needs and show both the original version and your edited version to your boss – this shows initiative. If you are planning to progress into your manager's shoes one day, it is important that you learn to think more strategically and see the bigger picture. This can sometimes involve spending more time to get to the bottom of it all, but your thinking should be that you need to do what is best for the firm.

Pressured times

We all experience work pressure and your boss is no different. They will be conducting their own work and probably supervising the work of a number of others. If your boss is going places in your organisation, then he/she will also be helping to manage his boss's workload too. Think about what you can do to release some of that pressure from them. Can you cover a meeting for them? If he/she is in meetings all day, can you grab them some lunch when you go to get your own? Are there people he/she needs to see to ask a few questions that you can take care of for them? Is there any research that needs doing? Can you create basic documents he/she needs so that they just need to tweak it rather than create something themselves from scratch? Let your boss know that you are happy to help if they think about anything extra you could do for them. Choose your moment carefully if you need advice or input from your boss. If they are flat out working towards a deadline, it probably isn't the right time to ask a small question. First thing in the morning or at the end of the day seems to net the best results. Small talk should be saved for when the pressure is off.

Manage the to-do lists for you and your boss

Always have an eye on what your boss needs to do. One-to-one meetings with your boss are a must and a good way to ensure that you stay up to date with what's going on from your boss's perspective. You should not only turn up to meetings with your to-do list, but ensure there is a process whereby you discuss their key tasks. What are their top three priorities, what is keeping them awake at night from a work perspective? And what else is coming down the wire you might want some advanced warning on? Once you find these things out, offer to help where you think you could add value. In addition, if you are in meetings with your boss and they are given an action, offer to help with the action if you can, even if it's as simple as asking a PA to set up a further meeting, or obtaining the papers or data your boss will need to complete the action. Verbally remind your boss of things they need to do. Be mindful that you don't come across as managing them – ensure you offer to help in a way that gives them a choice as to whether they want your help or not.

Bring your boss solutions, not problems

Ideally you should have explored every opportunity to solve a problem before bringing it to your boss's attention. Don't delay if it's urgent. The last thing any boss wants is to find out from someone else that something has gone wrong or that they are the last to know, as it makes your boss look as if they are not communicating with their team. When you bring a problem to their attention, explain what you've done to get to the bottom of the problem and what you believe needs to be done as a next step towards resolving the issue. Don't just turn up and tell them something is broken.

Always think commercially

Whatever role you are in, treat the company money as if it's your own business. Think about what you would spend if this was your business or how you would economise and negotiate to get the best deals possible. Always consider the financial value of everything you do. For example, if you and two colleagues take two days to prepare a report that no one is reading or that doesn't add any value, it is a waste of company money and resources. Money doesn't just leave the company's balance sheet because you are physically purchasing things – people's time costs money too!

Volunteer for the unglamorous projects

You know that project that no one else wants to do but that has to get done? Well, take it, do it, do it well and don't complain about it. On many occasions, the relationships you build in an area you wouldn't normally find yourself in can open you up to other opportunities and help grow your network. Volunteering to take the job that no one else in the team wants shows bravery and willingness to see the bigger picture. So what if this isn't part of your existing role? Your boss needs it done and they should be grateful that you have offered to get involved if everyone else is running away. It also shows your boss that you are not a one-trick pony and that you are willing to stretch yourself beyond other boundaries.

Communicate, communicate, and communicate again

I cannot overemphasise the importance of communication: emails, calls, videoconferences, watercooler chat, and whatever other methods you can muster. Always tell your boss what you are getting up to in some form – it could be a start-of-week update or a two-minute phone call. Never hold back bad news, never let your boss walk into a meeting and find out something that you could have given him a heads-up on. Regular communication with your boss is key, but you need to find out what frequency and form of communication they prefer. Don't be afraid to ask.

GRACE UNDER FIRE

"I know God will not give me anything I can't handle. I just wish He didn't trust me so much" – Mother Teresa

There is not much I haven't seen in the corporate world in terms of difficult situations. Some of these I have been in the middle of personally, whereas others I have only observed uncomfortably. Observing the predicaments of others is sometimes just as painful as if you were going through it yourself, and often the only way you can help is by listening and supporting that individual.

I have not always handled my difficult situations well (remember the lunch flying in the canteen?), often thinking I was better equipped to fight back or negotiate than I actually was. Hindsight is a beautiful thing, and reflection on those situations over the years has brought to the surface a number of ideas on how the situations could have been handled more effectively. There are, however, also some difficult situations where to this day I'm still totally proud of how I handled myself, even if all did not end well. Those situations are usually the ones where I stood up for my own values and ethics in the decisions I made.

Given the ever-changing nature of the working environment, there are hundreds of different scenarios that challenge corporate workers on a daily basis.

From what I have seen, difficult situations in the workplace tend to fall into two main categories:

- Difficult situations caused by people

- Difficult situations caused by organisational change

The downstream effect of any difficult situation is rarely positive in the first instance, and sometimes it's only clear much later why things happened the way they did. It is important that you realise you are not alone; many of your colleagues within the organisation would have experienced similar challenges, whether they've chosen to talk about them openly or not.

It is very difficult to offer one-size-fits-all advice as different individuals will react differently depending on the situation and the nature of their personality. I can only reflect on my own experiences and perhaps offer a little advice on how I handled some particular situations, good and bad.

Dealing with people

Whether you have had a personal experience of dealing with a difficult individual or observed one, it is fair to say we all know they exist. In their book, *First Break All the Rules: What The World's Greatest Managers Do Differently*, authors Marcus Buckingham and Curt Coffman say that people don't leave jobs, they leave managers. In my experience, they sometimes leave difficult colleagues too.

If someone is making your life difficult at work for whatever reason, no matter how much you enjoy your job and like the firm you work for, this can have a major impact in terms of your motivation and productivity. The easy option would be to just leave and walk away, however that would be tragic especially if you stand some chance of progressing at that particular firm.

The key here is to be the bigger person and try to remedy the situation before it gets out of hand. There is no point ignoring it, as these situations rarely go away in their entirety. I have seen situations where team members just ignore each other, which isn't good for business or for their colleagues either.

My first piece of advice would be to pause and try to understand the individual a bit better. Observe them. What are their triggers? Are there particular times/situations when they seem more difficult than others? Do they act differently in front of other people or are they different with different people? Are they just difficult for no reason, eg. because they can be due to a position of authority they hold, or do they just have a style that is not to your liking? Are you the only one who finds them difficult? It may seem a bit unfair to ask you to spend any time thinking about an individual that you have no time for, but it is important if you want to create a more tolerable relationship and working environment.

If you take time out to observe them over time, you may understand more about what triggers their behaviour and their personality traits that you find challenging. In turn, you will be better equipped to deal with any situations you may face in relation to this particular individual.

There is a point at which it should stop being something you think about. If they are exhibiting really unprofessional behaviour (eg. bullying or aggression) then you must address it, either with the individual directly, with the appropriate management team, or with HR. Twice I have allowed bullies to operate around me because I didn't recognise that their behaviour was in fact classic bullying. It was only when a colleague sent me a link to a site that detailed the traits of a bully that I realised their behaviour was officially unacceptable. A good place to visit for advice and information in those situations is the Advisory, Conciliation and Arbitration Service: www.acas.org.uk.

I vowed from that point on never to allow myself to be bullied or to allow others to be bullied in my presence. In the last instance of bullying I witnessed in the workplace, I actually raised it directly with the individual. They were totally shocked when I called them on it – they thought it was just a bit of fun and humour directed towards someone they had known for a while, and had absolutely zero awareness that it had made not only the individual to which it was directed feel extremely uncomfortable, but that it was having an effect on that person's colleagues too.

Having that conversation was difficult. However, with most difficult conversations and before you even book a meeting with the individual, you should take some time out to consider examples that relate to the subject you need to discuss, think about your approach to bringing it up, where you will have the conversation and the desired outcome. You may also wish to consider the individual's potential responses and how you will react in each situation so that the situation doesn't escalate out of control.

If anyone is being particularly difficult and you feel the situation may escalate at some point, you should have also started to keep a record of the instances where you have felt this person was being particularly difficult or situations that made you feel uncomfortable. Before you base your conversation around these instances, be totally honest with yourself: were they really being difficult or is this just your perception? Were they having an off-day or is it the case that every day with this individual turns into an off-day?

Under no circumstances should you rally your colleagues behind you, which may seem counterintuitive, but if they have issues then they should take them up themselves. Don't be the department's spokesperson just because no one else is brave enough to do it. Again, I fell into this trap once, and when the time came, the army of individuals that were goading me on to tackle this individual, the very ones who gave me all the examples to share, were in fact nowhere to be seen on the day! My point is, if you want to deal with a situation, do it based on your own sense of doing the right thing, and if it benefits others, then great.

Corporate protocol (although not documented or taught) would suggest that you try to tackle the situation directly with the individual in the first instance. Again, plan your conversation beforehand, base it on the notes you have taken and run it through with a trusted non-biased confidant outside your work environment. No names either when you're talking to a third party, as this does always work out to be a very small world!

It is really important that you try to strip any emotion out of your conversation. This is business, so keep it factual and professional. I would always advise having these conversations out of the office over a coffee, so if it does go horribly wrong at least you are not in full view of your colleagues or line manager. However, if this is a formal line management conversation you should look to have it in the office with a member of HR present.

When having the conversation, try not to include any personal snipes, no matter how sorely tempted you are. Should they snipe at you, acknowledge what they have said with a soft nod, maintain eye contact and move on with the rest of the conversation. Be aware of your body language here, as a soft nod with no expression versus a soft nod with raised eyebrows and a smirk may just as well have been a provocative verbal response.

On the topic of body language, this is not a conversation to have leaning back nonchalantly in your chair. Sit up straight like you mean business and open the conversation warmly with an intro of why you felt the conversation was needed.

At no time during the conversation should you lean across the table to appear confrontational. The best bet is to lean your forearms on the table in front of you or in your lap and hold your own hands; this will prevent you from becoming over-animated. I have always taken a notebook into these meetings with a framework of what we need to discuss – but never the full points, these are best memorised.

You should also be aware of the tone and pitch of your voice.

It is easy for emotion to take over during these conversations. It is far better to adopt a more monotone conversation than to show aggression through raised voice levels or pitch.

Articulate your points slowly and clearly, using factual cause and effect statements:

- Every time I am in a meeting and I speak up, you seem deliberately unsupportive of my ideas in front of everyone else (*THE CAUSE*)

- This is making me feel uncomfortable about putting my ideas forward because I am already anticipating a negative comment from you regardless of what I say (*THE EFFECT*)

- I was hoping we could discuss this and work out if there is an issue and how we can both move forward (*A SOLUTION*)

Then sit back and listen.

The key here is not to give the individual the reaction they were expecting. Stay focused on a positive outcome at all times. Two people not getting on doesn't benefit anybody, let alone the firm. You may have to eat a bit of humble pie and accept the fact the difficult person isn't someone you would ever socialise with; however, if they are going to be permanently in your working environment then you need to hold out the olive branch and try to make an effort to get along.

If the conversation ends in silence, thank them for their time and suggest that you get back together in the next day or so once they've had a chance to reflect. If you hear nothing, approach again, but no more than twice. Don't give up until you reach the point where you feel you can honestly do no more.

Never get into difficult conversations or follow-ups with individuals over email either. If you receive an email of this nature, reply politely and state you would much rather have the conversation face to face. That said, remember to retain all copies of emails just in case you might need them in the future. If the issues between you and this individual do escalate and HR gets involved, it is highly likely that copies of previously written communications will be requested, and the last thing you want is a whole herd of people reading what you said in frustration/anger or worse.

Dealing with difficult situations of a personal kind over the phone should also be avoided if possible. The best outcomes are achieved when two people are physically in each other's company. However, if this is not an option, then phone as opposed to email is the lesser of the two evils.

Never blind copy (BCC) your boss on emails either, or forward email chains that have taken place between yourself and the individual, unless you really feel there is an exceptional reason to do so and you are ready for HR to get involved in the dispute, as your line manager may immediately involve them if they deem the situation to be a risk. You should be able to articulate the conversations and situations well enough to your manager without using copies of personal conversations to prove a point. Should your manager want to see any email chains you refer to, then you should agree to the request.

There are instances where no amount of talking or scheduling meetings with the individual is going to remedy a situation. I have been there once myself and it wasn't a comfortable situation. Even though I am a relatively strong individual, dealing with a bully affected my health, confidence and performing my role to the best of my ability because my main focus was on surviving the day without an argument or unnecessary challenge.

Before you speak to your line manager you should formulate a couple of options as to what you'd suggest to remedy the situation (remember the tip on impressing your boss: always go armed with potential solutions). Think all options through before asking your boss for a one-to-one meeting to explain the situation. Again, you may wish to consider doing this out of the office if the difficult person works close by. Don't feel like you are telling tales if you have already approached the difficult person to no effect.

What if the difficult person is your boss?

The same approach applies. Make a note of situations where you feel the relationship is breaking down and how you could work together better. Be brave and tackle it with them sooner rather than later. Be open-minded to their opinions and thoughts too, none of us are perfect!

Don't be defensive when having these conversations, listen to what they have to say and consider your responses. Sometimes it is best to say nothing and then take time afterwards to think your responses through. Again, I would suggest trying to remedy the situation several times before taking drastic action like escalating the situation by involving HR or leaving your company entirely.

Don't wait for your performance reviews to have these types of conversations with a difficult boss or someone in your team. Tackle the issue head-on once you have given it some thought. Don't let a situation arise where your working relationship starts to affect your performance or, worse still, has an impact on your health or motivation.

On a final note, and again I speak from experience on this one, do not assume that you are to blame for the relationship failing or assume that because the difficult individual is your boss/ someone more senior to you that they are automatically right. In the case of your boss or a more senior individual being problematic, the way the game is played is that regardless of whether or not you agree with their perception of you as a person, your performance or their interpretation of a certain situation, they are still in a position of authority and, whether you like it or not, while you work for them your career at that particular firm is probably still in their hands. Again, there is lots of free advice and information to be found on the great site that is ACAS; you may wish to read through some of the white papers on this site before having these conversations.

If you feel the situation or relationship really is insurmountable for whatever reason, then you may wish to look at transferring to another part of the firm or perhaps even leaving the organisation. Remember, even if you transfer or leave there is always a likelihood that you will come across this individual again, either within your firm or outside it if you stay in the same sector or geographic location.

Dealing with the politics

I have worked with a number of individuals who are skilled politicians, albeit workplace politicians. They use their networks and a number of underhand skills to further their careers and personal agendas. They can't be avoided, and the further up the ladder you go in your career, the more prevalent they are, given that there is more power to be wielded higher up. I can offer no advice on how to deal with them beyond telling you to just be aware that they are there and observe how they operate so that you understand the rules of engagement if you end up having to deal with them directly.

Political animals and politics in general are part of every organisation, not just corporations. You can either choose to play the game or you can choose to sit and watch. The fact is that if you want to get ahead you need to be politically savvy. This doesn't mean that you need to adopt any bad behaviours yourself, it just means that you will have to learn to become more than a bystander.

Dealing with organisational change

A number of different scenarios can arise during your career due to organisational change. More often than not, you will have no say in the change and will invariably find yourself in the midst of it or at the end of a short stick. I often hear people saying in interviews how they embrace change and I say it too. The truth of the matter is that we will happily embrace change as long as it's for the good or if it's not affecting us in a major way, but we start to get nervous when it goes beyond that.

The gravity and impact of change means different things to different people. A change in line manager may actually be a good thing if you consider what we were discussing previously or if you've worked together for a long time without seeing significant progress. However, if you get on particularly well with your line manager and you have a productive working relationship, a change in line manager can be extremely difficult.

One thing for sure is that there will always be change in corporations. It goes with the territory. The key for you is working out how changes in the workplace will affect you most, both in terms of your career and home life. I was once faced with a change of line manager due to a restructure, and my new line manager was not necessarily a supporter of working from home. I felt that should I be asked to work a five-day week in the office again by the new manager, this change would be too much for me and my family in terms of the balance I had managed to establish between work and home. I was willing to meet them halfway, and I said that there were odd occasions where I could work in the office on a Friday, but this would have to be prearranged in order for me to source childcare. I also stated that if the five-day work week in the office was likely to become a more permanent expectation, then I would have to consider my options and whether I wanted to stay with that firm.

Redundancy

Another big change you may face is redundancy. Over the course of my career I have seen many individuals be made redundant, including my bosses. I have also observed the many different responses that people have had to being made redundant. Some have embraced it, especially if they are expecting a decent package due to long service. I have seen some people go into sheer panic at the prospect of losing their jobs, as they are either terrified at losing their paychecks and are insecure about their prospects of finding a new job, or sometimes it's even because their entire identity and self-worth has been wrapped up in doing their job with that particular firm and they don't know how to cope without that all-important business card. And some people have just taken it in their stride. Regardless of how it happens, it's not a nice situation to be in. However, if it gives hope to those that are currently going through this situation, I should mention that I can't think of a single instance where either friends, ex-colleagues or mentees who were made redundant haven't gone on to bigger and better things.

As an additional piece of advice around redundancy, if your situation is outside of the normal parameters, eg. you were made redundant just before bonus time or you were on maternity leave, you may wish to take legal advice to ensure you're getting the right deal. Legal advice doesn't have to be expensive and in certain circumstances you can actually request that your firm covers the cost. Again, more advice is available via www.acas.org.uk or from your local Citizens' Advice Bureau.

The positive side to redundancy is it does make you re-evaluate your career options and rethink your plans. I know a number of individuals who after being made redundant actually chose not to go back into corporate life, but decided to set up their own businesses or consultancies. I might add a few of them not only look 10 years younger, but they have also been very successful in their new endeavours.

Whether you fear redundancy or not, it is always best to keep your CV up to date. Always build a peer network both inside and outside your firm and never put the phone down on an approach from a headhunter or recruitment agent. You should always listen and build relationships with these individuals – you never know when you or someone close to you might need them.

I draw this advice not only from my own experience but from a situation I witnessed with a senior individual a few years back. This person was exceptionally well established at the firm they worked for and had been with the firm for over 20 years. They were the go-to person in the organisation, someone who knew how everything worked and who had all the key relationships at their fingertips. There was an organisational change and the CEO was removed from their post. A new CEO came in and did what most leaders do: they swept the place clean and this individual was pushed out with the dust as they were perceived as being part of the old guard rather than the way forward. This individual had no network outside of that organisation and hadn't updated their CV in 20 years. I got a phone call from this person in a sheer panic – they had no idea where to start!! I am happy to say that after nine months this individual managed to land themselves a new role and is now very happy; however, it shouldn't have taken that long given their experience.

The change overture

So we know that change happens, and we know that most textbooks tell us to embrace it, however it is not always as simple as that. There is no magic piece of advice I can offer when dealing with change as there are too many variables. Personally I have always tried to see the opportunity in the process. That opportunity may take a while to surface and you have to see it as part of your journey; however, accepting that things are out of your control (should that be the case) and getting on with it are key. See any positives you can muster and see where the wind takes you. As long as you are still getting paid, you have time to plan for any eventualities and hopefully can make more robust decisions.

The worst thing you can do is whinge about change and infect others around you, especially if you are leading a team. If there are decisions you can make so as not to feel the full impact of the change, then weigh them up and execute the ones that work for you. Alternatively, if you are not prepared to compromise, then consider your decisions and lead the change as opposed to being affected by it.

I have been in three organisations that have merged. When the incoming organisations have marched in, in metaphorical terms I have offered them tea. I have embraced them with positivity as I saw I had nothing to lose by trying. It's the same with new line managers; I have always given them the benefit of the doubt until they prove otherwise.

Change can be scary, but it is a massive learning opportunity too, both in terms of career and personal growth. My advice to you is to remain as upbeat as you can possibly be, plan in advance for all eventualities and the aspects you can control, ride with it and see where it leads you.

Results of dealing with difficult situations, namely stress

Change can lead to stress in multiple areas of your life. This can surface in a multitude of ways. You may feel like checking out or just powerless because you have no control over the changes you face. Other times it can lead to a total lack of motivation, or worse still, health issues. In some instances, organisational change can affect your financial stability in the case of redundancy or reduced hours. You can only plan for so many eventualities, and in some cases you don't even realise you are suffering from stress until it is already parked in your driveway.

If you suffer from constant recurring illnesses, tiredness, feelings that you cannot deal with the simplest of things, sleep changes and changes in your overall behaviour during periods of change at work or periods of significantly increased workloads, then I implore you to seek the relevant help and advice.

There have been times when I ignored more than one symptom early on in my career – I felt that if I admitted I felt stressed this would be a failure on my part. I used to bottle things up in my quest to appear strong to family, friends and work colleagues. Invariably, I was not able to maintain the pretence for too long and the end result would manifest itself in grand style, albeit in private. I regret those times and I regret not reaching out for the help I needed.

I am now better at knowing my limits. If I see the signs of stress making their way into my life, I pull back and try to regain some form of balance. I am no longer frightened to ask for help and don't see it as a dent in my pride if I cannot win the race by myself.

If it's your career that's giving you issues then seek the help of a mentor, confidant or coach. If it's stress in terms of health, don't delay in visiting your GP. I am no medical expert, but through countless bouts of ignorance I have learned over the years to listen to my body. It is often my body that pipes up with stress signals long before my mind admits that I may need a break.

My advice here is to listen to your body, know your triggers and try to identify the signs of stress sooner rather than later – and above all, seek the help you need, whether that's support from family, friends, work or that of professionals. There is no grand prize for being a martyr and attempting to deal with these situations on your own. Again, there is lots of advice on the ACAS site and also via the NHS and Health and Safety Executive website (www.hse.gov.uk).

NETWORKING FOR SUCCESS

"It's not what you know but who you know that makes the difference" – Anonymous

Networking is often something people find especially hard to do. So what's the point? It's all about chewing the fat and having drinks with people you don't really know – much better to spend the time being excellent at your job and delivering stuff, right? Well, perhaps not.

Building a successful career is as much about who you know (and who knows you) as it is about doing a good job. Get rid of the word 'networking' for a moment and replace it with 'the art of career development' or 'developing key relationships'. That's why anyone who cares about their career should care about networking and invest time in it. You are simply keeping people informed about what you do, what you are good at and how you can help them. Think about it as being what your boss and others need to know about you, above that you do a good job.

It's about the value of long-term relationships. Our careers start between the age of 16 to 25 and finish around age 50 to 65. Most people spend about 80% of their career in the same field. Therefore, you will end up knowing some of the same people for most of your career. Your reputation and theirs are based on the same journey over a significant number of years. If you are developing and nurturing relationships with these people for the long haul, it will help your career no end. This is where trust, reputation and personal brand comes from.

We also need to network externally, not just with the people in our own companies. What's the difference between networking internally and networking externally? You're still talking to people about what you're good at and how you can help them. Your focus externally will be on what you want networking to do for you. Networking with external contacts can be about your career development, personal development, building your profile, gathering competitor intelligence or customer intelligence, or maybe even about pursuing a passion a million miles away from work to help you blow off some steam!

A lot of relationship building can take place at events where there are lots of people, and that's the bit of networking that most people find particularly daunting. There are many tips for working a room, and you can find out how to learn this dark art by visiting my good friend Heather White's site here: www.smarter-networking.com.

As with most things, the more you do it, the better you get. At first you may feel out of your comfort zone but you will soon find your flow. It helps to remember that probably 50% of the people in the room are feeling exactly the same way you are.

A question I am often asked is whether it's OK to go to events and just hand out business cards to all and sundry. In the appropriate context, handing out your business card to someone you've just had a great chat with who wanted to follow up with you is absolutely the right thing to do. What you need to consider is when **NOT** to do it. There is no point in handing out your card if you haven't established a good connection between you and the other people in the group (or the person you are speaking to). Otherwise you might be seen as superficial, pushy, and sales-like and you want to avoid leaving the wrong impression with people. If you haven't connected with them, we can almost guarantee where your card and brand and reputation will end up – in the bin. Just think about how you feel if someone you barely know hands you their card – are you inspired to do anything with it? How would the conversation need to have gone to inspire you to want to connect with that person again? That's the conversation you need to be having. Unless you have managed to have that quality of conversation with everyone in the room, don't give everyone there your business card, it's as simple as that.

Another thing I get asked is why men don't need to network. They do need to network. They just tend to do it a bit differently from women, and most of the time it's second nature. Their networking interactions happen at the watercooler, on the golf course, in the pub, or wherever they are. A recent survey conducted by Smarter Networking with a group of men showed that they don't even really acknowledge networking as something they think about as a skill. Passing along recommendations, introducing contacts, and suggesting others for a job is done naturally and has no official label.

If you ever watch men at networking events, most of them can work the room and pick up contacts almost effortlessly. As with all things, there are also some men who are terrible at it and some women who seemed to be born knowing what to do. My advice is don't try to emulate their style or anyone else's for that matter, just focus on what makes you different or stand out in the crowd. Are you approachable? What networking style would work for you? Stay focused on what you want networking to do for you and just get on with it. In the end it all comes down to the same stuff – great results and great experiences.

Networking as a skill and a means to an end is far more diverse and adaptable than most have given it credit for. People often ask if there is a business case for networking. I can think of several benefits of networking:

- Opens career doors

- Helps find new employees

- Builds a peer group and provides support for others too

- Develops personal (and interpersonal) skills

- Develops self-marketing skills

- Opens doors to a wider variety of industry insights

- Generates new ideas from listening to people, and provides a forum to test ideas

- Displays abilities and raises profile

What are the main concerns when people first consider networking?

- You may feel uncomfortable approaching new people, especially if you are shy

- It can take a lot of time to get started

- Some events have distinct 'in-house cliques'

- It might be difficult to justify the time to the boss (if in office hours)

- It means time away from home (if out of office hours)

- You may not get the results you want

- The impact can be difficult to measure

- Other people may not respect confidentiality if you are networking to find another role

What do you want to achieve by networking? Maybe it's about:

- Developing better career opportunities

- Developing a network of alliances, partnerships and contacts

- Getting departments talking to each other and being more effective (culture change)

- Tapping into the crossing-selling opportunities inside an organisation

- Becoming a better *internal* consultant

- Setting up internal networked groups, eg. receptionists, support teams, similar teams across different business lines

- Improving self-marketing skills

- Sharing knowledge more easily and readily

- Gaining market information and sharing the intelligence effectively

- Generating new clients

- Getting more out of attending conferences, exhibitions and forums

The whole reason I set up www.wearethecity.com was to promote networking and the thousands of different networking organisations that exist, not just in the UK but all over the world. The site includes a directory that will open your eyes to many different networking groups by industry, ethnic group, sexual orientation, for entrepreneurs or for people in corporate careers. I wish I had discovered the power of networking 10 years earlier than I did as it would have been great to get those opportunities to learn new skills, build my peer groups and also utilise the support through those networks when times were tough.

In true form I leveraged my own network in order to learn how to be better at it. I sought and still continue to seek the advice of the legend that is Carole Stone, the Institute of Directors' most connected woman, Heather White of Smarter Networking and Andy Lopata of Connecting is Not Enough at: http://www. lopata.co.uk/. Leveraging their advice, I developed my own approach to networking and am able to teach others, spreading the word to the hundreds of individuals I meet through my own speaking and networking activities each month.

Having an extensive network enabled me to help find jobs for 23 people last year and put 20 children into work experience, and that's not to mention the massive amount of money my network has helped me to raise for charity. My networking and my network have also helped me to build the businesses of others and grow future business owners and leaders. Without my network, and the time and investment I put into it, I would not be able help so many people to achieve their goals, who in turn have helped me to achieve my own.

I have been told I am a 'connectpreneur' and one of the most well-networked women in the City of London (bear in mind it's just a square mile, albeit an important one), and I take that as a huge compliment. I am not a fan of labels, however what is true is that I do have an extensive network which also includes a number of other individuals who are extensively networked. This multiplier effect makes my network even stronger and my ability to connect to people much greater.

I have invested the last six years in growing my network. I maintain it through face-to-face meetings, emails, Skype and through various different social media tools. It takes time and it takes effort, but it reaps rewards. If there is only one thing you do after reading this book I suggest networking should be it.

Top tips for networking

- Ensure you have a strong introduction in terms of your opening lines. Make sure you give the people you meet enough hooks in your opening sentences so they can easily make a conversation based on the number of different facts you drop about yourself. For example, if you start with: "Hi, I'm (insert name here). I'm the (insert current role) at (insert current company). This is my (Xth) time at an event with this network, how about you?", this allows people to respond: "Wow, what an interesting name – where are you from?" or "Wow, I'm a (your current role) too, how long have you been doing that?" or "My neighbour works at (your current company), do you know John Smith in the finance department?" or "I'm brand new to this network. What else can you tell me about it?" And from there your conversation is off and running.

- Vary your networking activities so you meet different kinds of people. Don't just stick to your industry networks, go and discover other networks. For instance: if you are a woman in a marketing function in a retail bank, have a look at some generic women's networks, groups for marketing professionals across sectors, and groups for the retail banking sector to ensure you get a good cross section of ideas relevant to different aspects of who you are and what you do. Don't forget to include something for any personal interests too; if you are passionate about running, then a running club is another fantastic way to make some diverse connections and get some exercise at the same time. Job done!

- Always follow up with the people you connected with within 48 hours of meeting them via whichever channel you think is the most appropriate, whether that's LinkedIn, email, telephone, or stopping by somebody's desk if they are internal. Again, you're not following up with every single person you were introduced to, just the people you sparked with that you want to engage with again. This is not about racking up your number of connections on LinkedIn – if you'll never have a reason to speak with them again then there's no point in establishing that connection.

- Relationships are not transactional. Ensure you keep in contact with your contacts periodically, not just when you want or need something.

RAISE YOUR OWN PROFILE

"You are your own Chief Marketing Officer, go sell" – Tom Peters

From a cultural perspective we are not taught to sing our own praises or talk about our successes. I would like to challenge a few aspects of that status quo within this chapter. I am often asked if raising your profile is also seen as boasting, and my answer is it depends on how you frame your profile-raising activity and the words you use.

What is profile? Is it the same thing as reputation or brand? For me it's about three things:

What people see – *The visual image of a person*

What people hear – *A verbal description of a person*

What people say – *The opinions of others*

There are many ways of raising your profile. You could put your face up on a billboard or at a bus stop, but let's face it, not many people would be comfortable with that. There are also people in the public eye that have a great deal of profile, but they may also have huge PR teams behind them. The question is how can you do your own PR, raise your profile, and overcome what is probably the biggest barrier around this – feeling comfortable about it?

If by this point you have created a mission statement with your strategy and goals and tasks all mapped out, have a look over the entire thing and see where there might be opportunities to raise your profile in line with those activities. If you don't see the opportunities, this is a good time to involve friends and mentors to get their input. I bet there are lots, but the bigger question is will you take them up and maximise the potential that lies within those opportunities?

Promoting yourself in either a written or verbal format takes a bit of courage. The fear of being judged by others takes a while to get over, and because of this a lot of people choose to stay in the background. When you put yourself out there you are invariably opening yourself up for other people's opinions; however, it depends on how far you want to take your profile-raising activities. For example, some people find it difficult just to complete their LinkedIn profile in any kind of detail, worrying that they will be perceived by their colleagues to be 'bragging', even when all of the achievements they'd include are absolutely legitimate. For me personally, I have turned down opportunities to be on television in the past, because I know that I wouldn't necessarily be comfortable with that level of exposure, even though I am totally OK with being present on the internet and on various social media channels in a significant way. Everyone is different. People like to be recognised; however, without someone raising your profile for you, there is an element of it that you have to do yourself.

I still feel uncomfortable with certain aspects of it to this day. Every time I present my Power of Profile talk or other training sessions, my first slide talks about my awards and what I have achieved. I include this slide as the first one on purpose, not because I want to sing about my success, but because it enables me to share with my audience that no matter how many times I present this part of my session, there are times when I still feel uncomfortable talking about my success stories. I know, however, that it is important to establish my credibility with an audience on the topic of profile if I want to keep getting referrals to do more talks. Therefore, there has to be an element of self-promotion if I want to achieve my goals and overall mission of getting my name out there as a subject matter expert in helping corporate women navigate their careers. If I don't establish myself as an SME in this space, it means my plan to exit corporate life by the time I am

45 (remember my mission earlier) won't happen, therefore I accept that there is an element of doing my own PR that I need to engage in to get ahead.

With women in particular, there seems to be an overwhelming urge to follow up every profile-raising or complimentary statement we make about ourselves with a self-deprecating comment. It must be something in our DNA. Have you ever received a compliment from someone about what you are wearing, and your response is: "Oh, this old thing?" or "It was the first thing in the closet." I was taught a long time ago by another coach just to say thank you and take the compliment, not to try to deflect it with a disposable sentence which can actually make the person giving the compliment feel a bit silly for having said anything in the first place. One of my American friends has pointed out that this tendency to talk ourselves down may also be a particularly British trait, as Americans in general seem much happier to wax lyrical about their achievements, so don't forget to factor in any necessary cultural overlays in your thinking on the topic too.

So if we have trouble taking a compliment from someone else, it's obvious how difficult we find it actually talking about ourselves in a complimentary way, but it is something you must learn to do if you want to raise your profile. I believe there is a way that you can overcome your internal barriers and raise your profile, but the importance lies in how you do it: what you say, when you say it and who you say it to. In today's world of social media, you also need to consider what tools are the most appropriate to raise your profile, as written text can be interpreted very differently from verbal conversation. It is easier for comments to be misinterpreted in social media, especially on something like Twitter where the restriction on the number of characters you can use may mean that you can't explain something quite the way you normally would. My advice is that you should still leverage social media tools, but know their limitations and proceed with the appropriate level of caution.

Think of it like this. Every time you network, whether you do that online or in the real world, you are effectively raising your profile. Every time you tweet or add something to LinkedIn and tell others what you are doing, you are effectively raising your profile. Every meeting you attend and every event you go to with other people is an opportunity to raise your profile. Every project you volunteer for is an opportunity to raise your profile.

Profile-raising is about being seen/having your name seen (eg. the networking piece) and it is about having your content heard (the profile piece).

From a career perspective, it is important that you learn to become more comfortable with the art of speaking up and telling people more about yourself and what you have achieved. In the corporate world, line managers change and whole jobs and departments get moved or disappear, in which case it is very easy to lose aspects of your story. It's important to use a variety of mechanisms to keep your story alive and ensure that key points of it are heard, or better still, repeated by others. This has become much easier to do on your own with the introduction of different social media platforms.

Using social media to raise your profile

How should you talk about yourself on social media? There is nothing wrong with posting an update to Twitter or LinkedIn, or Facebook for that matter, telling others what you are up to. It's more about knowing who your audience is on a particular channel and the way you word your update that counts. For instance, there may be some of your activities that your family may be really proud of, but do your colleagues and professional contacts need to know that you and your children won the Most Perfectly Decorated Easter Egg contest at school?

On the more professional social media tools liked LinkedIn and Twitter, it is more acceptable to talk about your professional achievements or for entrepreneurs to promote their products and services. I use both of these tools daily and am often speaking about what I have been up to. I intersperse my own updates with updates from other people in my network as well, which helps us both by making others aware of who I'm connected to while also supporting the endeavours of the other people in my network.

Here's an example. Let's say I want to post an update about an event that I am speaking at in order to raise my own profile around my public speaking. My client's name is pretty impressive and I am hoping that this speaking engagement will lead to more speaking engagements. How would I proceed? Where would I post it?

Facebook? Probably not, as my Facebook account is restricted to purely family and friends, there are no clients or colleagues connected to me on there. Would this update really interest them or lead to anything else for me? Unlikely.

Twitter? Yes, as there could be potential new clients following me, plus I know that my client also uses Twitter, and if they follow me, they will invariably see my tweet which shows that I am helping to promote their event as well.

LinkedIn? Yes, as I am connected to a number of people from organisations I would like to speak at. But on the caution front, I have to be careful about what I say here, as I am also connected to the senior management team from my day job and I don't want them to think I performed this talk during work time.

Pinterest? Potentially, but it absolutely depends on my audience for this particular talk.

The key here is considering what platforms to use and how to tailor your message for each audience. And if you can raise the profile of someone else before raising your own, go for it. Using my previous example, that might look like this:

Twitter: Big thank you to @xxxxx for giving me the opportunity to speak to their fab audience this eve, really enjoyed it, gr8 org.

LinkedIn: Great dialogue with the audience speaking for XX last night, if you want to find out more about this dynamic organisation, see this link.

Pinterest: See link to fab event I was lucky enough to speak at (attach picture).

With my various updates I have managed to tell others what I have been up to, and I have also managed to raise the profile of the organisation that hired me to speak. In turn, I feel more comfortable raising my own profile as I am promoting someone else's profile simultaneously.

What tends to happen in terms of these profile-raising activities is that they are then promoted by the individuals whose profile you have also raised. They may have wanted to do it themselves but felt too uncomfortable, so it is easier to spread something good that someone else has said about you rather than doing it yourself. Going back to my example, here's what that looks like. I will tweet my thank you via Twitter, the organisation I have thanked will probably retweet my thanks to their followers, and then I get more followers as a consequence. People will notice my update on LinkedIn and potentially comment and share it with their network (if it's interesting to them). In addition, I may well have posted my update to the various groups I follow or own, which then leads to more comments and shares, all of which equals lots of profile-raising for the company I originally spoke for.

There are ways to raise your profile within your organisations too, even if your organisation is one which shuns social media use. You could set up a lunch-and-learn, attend as many internal networking events as possible, attend meetings in other areas as I mentioned earlier in the book, or get involved in charity initiatives or programmes internally where they are looking for volunteers. There will be other ways as well, so be creative and, again, you might want to talk to colleagues to get some other suggestions for what might work in your firm. If you can get your corporate communications department to be aware of everything you are involved in, that's even better – get stories on the company intranet or offer to speak at events that may be on their radar. The more you do, the more of a story you have to tell.

In addition to using social media, externally you could join and perhaps even volunteer to help out at a network (they are always looking for helpers), you could write your own blog or set up your own website. You could write articles for magazines or other sites. Most of the 300 writers we have on WeAreTheCity did exactly that – they wrote in to our site with a sample story and we gave them a profile by including them on our site.

I personally recommend having your own website. Buying your first name/surname domain (eg. vanessavallely.com) should be top of your list even if you never use it – who knows, in the future someone with the same name as you may become famous before you do and want to buy it from you for millions! Website domains have become really cheap and can be easily purchased over the internet. Setting up your website is important too, even if it is just a place for you to blog (I find WordPress to be the best tool for websites and blogs). A number of entrepreneurial networks run courses on setting up your website.

Top tips for raising your profile:

- Don't be frightened to tell others what you have achieved, just be conscious of how you word it

- Ensure you have a strong LinkedIn profile, a good head shot and a bio (a shorter CV) if you require one

- Invest time in LinkedIn and social media, tell others what you are doing, but again be careful how you word your updates – think about your different audiences

- Use your network/mentors/champions to help raise your profile

- Always promote the profile of others before your own

- Buy yourself a domain name on the web and set up your own website

- Get involved with internal activities within your corporate environment

- Offer to write for websites, internal intranets or anywhere where you could add value with your subject matter expertise

FIND YOUR MENTORS, CHAMPIONS AND COACHES

"I am not a teacher, but an awakener" — Robert Frost

There are lots of different types of people who can help you under lots of different names, which can get a bit confusing. I frequently have people asking me who exactly it is that they should be getting support from. Let me give you my definitions for the sake of clarity.

Mentor

A *mentor* is someone who is more skilled or experienced than you who offers advice, support and guidance to facilitate learning and development.

Champion

A *champion* is someone who promotes you and your capabilities for the right opportunities. They are sometimes also described as sponsors. These are individuals who have the ability to open doors for you when you are not in the room and potentially even help create opportunities for you. These individuals are well connected in the areas you want to get into and know enough about you to champion your work, achievements and ability. Champions can be previous mentors, but there's an important distinction: as a mentor they would have just been talking to you about you, but as a champion they are shouting about you from the rooftops to other people.

Coach

A coach is an individual who assists people with identifying specific goals and then reaching those goals faster and with ease. Think of the sports comparison – an Olympic runner's coach is responsible for making the runner get to the finishing line as fast as possible, and will work with the runner on everything that contributes to that particular objective. A business coach would be similar, but your challenge might be more along the lines of getting their support around everything you need to think about to ensure you deliver a huge project on time and on budget.

During different times in your career you may need to engage the services of all three. However, I want to focus on the first two, as these are low cost and massively important in terms of your professional growth and career.

What are you looking for in a mentor?

Before approaching a potential mentor, you should be clear on what you are looking for. What do you want from the mentor? How long are you likely to need their support? How often do you think you need to meet? When you approach your prospective mentor you should be able to articulate your requirements clearly so they know what they are signing up for. Ideally a mentor should be someone who already has the skills, contacts or experience that you aspire to.

Seeking a mentor

You can seek your mentors from a variety of sources, either internally or externally. If you have grown your network and joined industry forums, your mentors should be relatively easy to find. You could also consider putting out a request for mentors via LinkedIn or Twitter.

A number of external networks also operate mentoring schemes, so these are worth investigating too. You should also contact your internal employee networks or your HR department to see if there are any mentoring schemes running internally.

Being a mentor

If you are looking to mentor, the Cherie Blair Foundation is running a large mentoring scheme and there are a number of other organisations that are crying out for mentors, especially in schools and colleges. This is a great way to give back, and I truly believe that mentors get as much out of a mentoring relationship as mentees do, as they get to look at situations through a different lens.

Don't be afraid to ask

If there is someone that you aspire to be like and you feel they would be the right individual to mentor you, then ask them! The worst that could happen is they say no, but you might get lucky! **Aim high**

Ideally you should have mentors both inside and outside your organisation. In an ideal world, these mentors should be at least one to two levels above your current position. Just because someone is very senior doesn't mean that they won't be prepared to mentor you, but you may have to provide a slightly more compelling case in order for them to give up their time. If you are approaching senior individuals to mentor you, you must be clear about the time that is required, always turn up prepared and make the most of the time you spend together.

Approach based on specific goals

Before you meet with your mentor, write down a few specific goals that you wish to achieve during your mentoring relationship. Ensure that you make these goals explicit during your first meeting and double check with your prospective mentor that they feel they can help you with what you are looking to achieve.

Agree expectations

Expectations must be set on both sides. You need to be clear on what a mentor is not going to do. They are not there to do your work for you, they are there to support you and guide you with their experience. It is important that you agree expectations up front, and this could also be in relation to the administrative aspects of the relationship like the frequency of your mentoring sessions, when is a good time to take phone calls, how quickly emails will be responded to and so on.

Source multiple mentors

You should try to source a few different mentors. As mentioned earlier, at least one should be internal and one should be external. I have always sought yet another mentor who is completely outside of my industry in order to give me a completely different view of my situation.

Costs

Mentoring relationships normally don't cost and can be informal. However, if you are engaging a professional mentor or coach there may be some costs associated with their time. Always check before entering the relationship.

Mentoring rules

- Turn up on time

- Turn up prepared

- Arrange the next session at the end of the present one

- Be prepared to be challenged

- Be open minded to new approaches

Mentors do not work for you nor are they usually being paid. Be respectful and appreciate that they are giving up their time in order to help you further your career, so never miss a mentoring session if at all possible.

Your responsibilities

- Determine your goals

- Approach your mentors

- Build the relationship

- Be open and honest with your challenges and previous experience

- Make the most of the learning opportunity

- Organise the meetings

Their responsibilities

- Commit to being your mentor

- Review and agree goals and commitment

- Share experience

- Listen and provide feedback

- Suggest alternative forms of learning

- Make introductions

Use technology

Your mentoring relationships may well be long distance, therefore you may wish to consider the use of technology tools such as Skype, or Dropbox for sharing files, or even Google Hangouts. Don't let your mentoring session slip just because you and your mentor cannot be in the same physical location.

Learn to mentor others

Your mentoring experience should also be an opportunity for you to learn how to mentor as well as being mentored. Observe your mentor in this capacity and then mix in your own style once you start to mentor others.

My personal mentoring rules

These are my personal mentoring rules and ones you may wish to adopt once you start to mentor other individuals:

- I won't mentor anyone who is not themselves mentoring the next level down, as otherwise my experience stops with me and my existing mentee.

- I won't commence a mentoring session unless I have seen a clearly articulated plan of what the mentee wishes to achieve. I want to be sure I am in fact the individual they need, and if I don't see a plan I can't know that for sure.

- Once I mentor an individual, I see it as my personal responsibility as their mentor to find them their next mentor when the time comes and I am no longer the right person to support them.

- Whoever I mentor, I also champion. I put their names forward for any appropriate opportunities that could potentially develop their careers.

Giving back via mentoring is an amazing way of helping to build future generations of talent. If you are considering being a mentor outside your organisation then I would recommend: http://getmentoring.org/ or http://www.mentoring.org/

What is a champion?

A champion is an individual who evangelises about you to the wider world. They understand your experience, your strengths and your aspirations in terms of your career or business.

What they should do

- Promote you at every opportunity (as long as your experience is fitting)

- Provide ad hoc mentoring advice when required

- Connect you to their network

- Be proactive in seeking new opportunities for you

- Provide spot challenges for you, or tasks that will take you out of your comfort zone

- Help you to grow your mentor/championing network

You don't generally find champions in the same way that you might find mentors as champions will tend to have had more direct exposure to your work in order to feel confident about promoting your work to others.

Ideally your champion should be well connected in the areas you aspire to. For any champion it is important that they understand you as an individual and that they have first-hand experience of your talent in the particular area they are promoting you for. Bear in mind their integrity is wrapped up in any opportunity they put you forward for, as any negative behaviour on your part could then reflect badly on them as the introducer.

If you are lucky enough to have found champions, your role is always to follow up on the opportunities they provide for you. If they are pushing you in a direction you don't wish to go, be honest with your champion and be explicit about the opportunities you would like to be considered for and those you wouldn't.

Regardless of whether you are talking to mentors, coaches or champions, be clear about the opportunities you are looking for and your areas of interest so that any of those people are well equipped to make the right introductions for you.

YOUR CAREER TOOLKIT - EVERYONE NEEDS ONE

Social Media - Career tools

LinkedIn - www.linkedin.com

LinkedIn is one of the most powerful tools you can use to both raise your profile and keep tabs on all your connections online. Millions of people are now on LinkedIn and if you are not one of them, then you are missing an important career trick.

LinkedIn is a place where you can detail your career experience and really paint a picture to either your connections or prospective employers.

Here are a few additional tips for building a strong LinkedIn profile and getting the most out of this amazing tool:

- **Your job title** – In the job title field, don't just detail your existing job title, but include other job titles you have held in the past. From a search engine optimisation perspective this field is optimised, therefore if you are a programme manager or have been and you don't have these words in the job title field, you won't appear high in the search for any individual who happens to be searching on those words.

- **Ensure you have a strong summary description** – This is your professional shop window, so take your time to write your summary and remember to sell yourself. Once again, this field is optimised from a search engine perspective, so you want to fill it with as many relevant words as possible that sum up you and your experience. If you have issues writing about yourself, a good exercise is to write about yourself in the third person. Don't just detail that you are hard-working and experienced, use juicy descriptors to paint a more detailed picture of your capabilities. Don't forget to add metrics to your descriptions like how many people you managed, the size of the budget you were responsible for, the sales figures you achieved, or how many months early you delivered your project versus a planned time frame of X. Think back to the cause and effect statements we used earlier – you should think about the same thing here. The project was to deliver A *(CAUSE)*, which enabled the business to do B *(EFFECT)*. As with any summary, if the reader likes what they see in the summary they are more likely to read on to the detail to find out more about you.

- **Have a good headshot** – When I say good headshot that means no pictures where your friends have been cut out of the photo or where you can see your auntie's flock wallpaper in the background. Invest in a decent headshot. You can get these done at most photo shops.

- **Meet and connect** – If you have been out networking, always ask the people you meet if they are on LinkedIn and if they would mind if you connected with them. When you do, always amend the standard text so it doesn't just say 'I would like to add you to my LinkedIn profile'. Ensure you detail where you met and, if appropriate, what you discussed to personalise the connection (and remind the person which one of the potentially many people they met you are). Above all, ensure you do this within 48 hours of meeting them.

- **Clear out** – You can regularly go through your LinkedIn connections and clear out the individuals you feel you can no longer help or those who will not benefit from your updates. Individuals do not get a message when you remove them from your connections.

- **Treat LinkedIn like your front door** – You should know or have met every individual in your LinkedIn network. If you get invitations from individuals you don't know, my advice is not to accept them unless you have met with them or interacted with them in some way. If you work hard to build your network like I have done, then why would you just open the front door and let anyone in? The same goes for your LinkedIn invitations, you should not be sending invitations cold. If you want to meet or connect with an individual, you can see who in your existing network knows them and ask for an introduction.

- **Keep your profile updated** – Keeping your LinkedIn profile up to date is an ongoing process. I probably update my LinkedIn at least twice a month, adding new experiences and skills and removing items that I feel are no longer relevant.

- **Use the update facility** – I use the update facility on LinkedIn at least once a week to update my contacts about the individuals I have met through networking and my key projects. Remember what I said earlier about using LinkedIn to promote the profile of others. I also use the update facility to ask for help and to call on the experience of others. I truly believe that there is no question I could ask of my network that they couldn't answer (or else they would know someone who could help).

- **Join groups/set up groups** – Groups are great, but as with connections, it is about quality rather than quantity. If you join a group, it should be because you are planning to participate in that group or you feel you could learn from the group's members. Always respect the group rules. Setting up groups is a great way of forming your own small network. There are various different group types you can set up and they are all very easy to use.

- **Request timely recommendations** – If you have worked with an individual and feel you have done a good job, then ask them to recommend you on LinkedIn. Again, these recommendations will help to build up a picture of your capabilities and experiences. I would also encourage you to write recommendations for others, don't wait to be asked. If someone has impressed you, then help to raise their profile by writing them a recommendation. It is up to them if they wish to show this on their profile, but I am sure they will appreciate the time you took to write it and the kind gesture.

Twitter - www.twitter.com

Twitter is a great tool for research, raising your profile, meeting new people and collaborating. I follow people who share the same interests as I do, therefore I get access to thought leadership, articles and views on subjects that I am really interested in through them, as well as things I find myself. News hits Twitter long before it hits the newsfeeds so Twitter has turned into my daily newspaper and I honestly couldn't live without it. It is worth keeping in mind that you carry your firm's brand with you at all times, so think about what your company would think about what you tweet before you post anything.

If you are thinking about using Twitter, my advice would be to create an account, follow a few individuals that interest you and just watch how it works for a little while before you wade in yourself. Watch what people are tweeting and how they interact with others. Once you have your account set up, these tips may help you:

- **Your picture, logo or image** – Ensure you have a picture on your Twitter profile, or your logo or even a cartoon avatar if you prefer. Never leave your account with the default egg image, people generally won't follow an egg as they can't be sure of who they are following.

- **A decent summary** – Ensure you also have a strong description in your Twitter profile summary and that you include links to your company if you are an entrepreneur. You only get a limited amount of characters to detail your summary, so choose your words wisely.

- **Follow like-minded individuals** – Follow individuals who interest you, and take a look at who they are following too. This is a good way of building up a more diverse list of people to follow, and that will give you access to a wider range of content and opinions to inform what you want to say and do.

- **Be careful what you tweet** – 140 characters to type it, 140 seconds to read it back. How will your tweet land with your audience? Never type a tweet in anger – I have watched this seriously backfire on people. Twitter is not a place to express strong opinions unless you are prepared to deal with the fact that responses may be extremely quick and you may not necessarily get the time to defend your opinion! Also, you may not be able to retract what you said, and what goes on the internet tends to stay on the internet, so mind what you say.

- **Tweet regularly** – Once you are comfortable with Twitter, ensure you tweet regularly. Don't just sit there and watch. Interact! It's the whole point of the tool, and it can work brilliantly.

- **Tweet interesting and relevant content** – Deep thoughts on Twitter are fine, but remember to add value to your followers by tweeting interesting and relevant content. Nobody wants to hear about what you had for lunch unless you've just been to the hottest new restaurant in town that you're trying to let everybody know about!

- **Build relationships** – Twitter is an amazing place to meet new people from around the globe. When you start to follow people or they start to follow you, at some point you may end up engaging in some form of dialogue with them. If your relationship has developed over a period of time, you may wish to meet them in person if they are local or connect with them at networking events or via LinkedIn. The normal safety and common sense rules apply when meeting anyone you don't know through a social media channel!

- **Promote others** – You can retweet interesting content from the people you follow to your own followers. And you can say thank you when anyone retweets you! If you meet someone through the course of your networking activities, ask for their Twitter name when you get their other contact details and give them a tweet after you have met, explaining who they are and what they do to your followers if you think they are someone of interest.

- **Avoid negativity** – When topics are trending it's hard to resist the lure of tweeting in with your opinion. I would strongly advise that getting involved with any form of negativity on any form of social media is a total waste of time, especially on Twitter as responses are far too quick for you to defend, and you can end up having to do damage control on your reputation for having done nothing more than posted a 140-character comment. Just think before you post anything, is it worth it?

Always keep your CV up to date

Your CV is not something that you get out and dust off every time you are worried about your job or are thinking of leaving. You should review it every three to six months, removing the irrelevant experience and adding new details to keep it up to date.

Your CV should have a strong summary (see advice for LinkedIn summary), and your jobs should be detailed with no gaps in between dates. If you have gaps then explain them. Responsibilities are sometimes easier to list as bullet points rather than writing in prose. Always include metrics in your explanations where you can, eg. how big was the department, was it global, what was the budget, what was the level of complexity of the jobs and what was the cause and effect of what you delivered?

I have probably reviewed thousands of CVs in my career, and I know there are a wide variety of opinions out there about what CVs should look like and what they should and shouldn't include. Personally I prefer to read the headlines about an individual on the first page before getting into the detail. Page 1 should give me their personal details, summary of their experience, key skills, qualifications and any other relevant high-level detail. From page 2 I want to see the details of their career experience. It is challenging to keep a CV short when you get further along in life if you have made a number of career moves, but do your best to stay brief – have sympathy for the people reading your CV who don't want to go through *War and Peace* to fill a role!

Other career must-haves:

Elevator pitch – This is your 60-second pitch should you meet the CEO of the company in the lift and he asks you what you do. You should think about practising this. Having this in your pocket ready to go is also very useful from a networking perspective, as the detail you include in your elevator pitch also serves as a useful introduction when meeting others.

Business cards – If you don't get business cards automatically as part of your role, then purchase your own – they are now very cheap to find on the internet. Remember to include all forms of contact information including your phone number(s), email address, Twitter handle, website URL and blog URL if you have them.

Style and substance – I am a true believer that people should be judged for their capabilities and what is inside their heads; however, the world we live in judges people by other things too, especially in a corporate context. People make up their mind about you within the first few seconds of meeting you. Being appropriately dressed and well turned out is paramount in the corporate world. Whatever the dress code is in your workplace, you should adhere to it. Some of the more creative sectors are more flexible about personal style and letting people display more individuality, but other sectors are quite strict about the need to conform to the norm of suits and dresses. This is not to say that you can't mix it up to bring a little more of your own individual style and brand to the picture. For example, I may well wear a suit, but I will always include something with my outfit that displays my personality, whether that's the colour of my shoes or shirt, a statement piece of jewellery, my handbag or some other accessory. I do shudder at the thought of how I dressed 10 years ago, I looked like a woman in a man's suit; at the time that was the persona I thought I needed to adopt in order to be accepted by my peers, but I think I was wrong! Now I am much more likely to embrace my feminine side and be proud that I am a woman, rather than treating it like something to hide!

GIVING BACK HELPS YOUR CAREER

I am a true believer in giving back to our communities. I also believe doing so is not only the right thing to do in terms of being a good citizen, but it opens your eyes to new skills, different networks of individuals and you learn new things as a consequence.

Giving back or helping charities or social enterprises is not just about handing over money (see http://www.reachskills.org.uk/). Many of these organisations are crying out for the skills of corporate workers to come and help their charities/social enterprises to be managed in a more business like fashion.

If giving back is something you would like to do, here are a few ideas of how you may wish to approach this worthwhile activity.

Become a school governor

Holding a school governorship is a great way to start your journey that may then lead to being a charity trustee and ultimately a corporate board member. Schools in the UK are crying out for governors who will play an active strategic role in helping to shape the school. For school governor positions in the UK, I would recommend visiting the National Governors Association or for actual positions, visit https://www.gov.uk/become-school-college-governor. It is an amazing thing to do and is extremely rewarding. Please note that a Criminal Record Bureau check (CRB) is a requirement of being a school governor.

Become a charity trustee

If you aspire to a board position at some point, you may wish to consider applying to be a trustee for a charity. Charities welcome a diverse range of business skills depending on what the charity does. There are a number of centralised organisations on the web that advertise trustee positions, however I recommend using http://www.trusteenet.org.uk/ for UK positions.

If you aspire to a trustee or board position, there are a number of different information sites that can help you, the latest is www.nonexechub.com. If you are female, there are also a number of networks that are trying to get more women on to boards in the UK. I would recommend finding out more via

http://www.womenonboards.co.uk/

Encourage the next generation

I believe it is our role to encourage and support the next generation of boys and girls in their careers. We can do this by giving our time (mentoring) or by sharing our stories (eg. going back to your old school). There are a number of organisations that will connect you to school programmes where you can help. Be aware that there are likely to be a number of checks that need to be performed (including a CRB) before you are able to work in schools in the UK.

YOUR CAREER CHECKLIST

- Introduce a **strategic review** into your life. Baseline where you are today, map your journey and monitor your progress quarterly – remember, that which can't be measured doesn't get done!

- **Keep focused** – Have a **mission**, a **plan** and a set of **goals** in whatever format works for you

- **Network, network, network** – Attend at least one networking event every month. **Connect** with the individuals you meet within 48 hours either via email or social media tools (eg. LinkedIn). Above all, **keep in touch** – don't just contact people when you want something

- **Ask** - I cannot emphasise this point enough. Ask **for help**, ask **for guidance**, ask **for experience and opportunities**, ask for **feedback**, ask for **mentors**, ask for **promotions**, ask for **pay rises** - if you don't ask, you don't get. Just remember for everything you receive, you must seek ways to give back to others in some way.

- **Be visible** – Invest time in **developing your LinkedIn profile, connections and recommendations**. Keep others aware of your activities using Twitter

- **Learn** – Constantly **seek opportunities** for learning/ self improvement

- **Get involved in mentoring** – Find yourself mentors and seek mentees

- **Find your champions** – Look for the people who will connect you to the right opportunities

- **Give back** – Always approach every conversation with **what I can give** to that individual, not what they can do for me. Good deeds will always come back! Consider getting involved with some other giving back activities like volunteer work with charities

- **Write to increase your profile** – Investigate somewhere you can blog or better still **create your own website**

- Ensure your **CV is up to date** and revise it at least every three to six months

ONE FOR THE LADIES - CAN WE REALLY HAVE IT ALL?

"I've learned that you can't have everything and do everything at the same time" – Oprah Winfrey

The most frequent question I am asked is how do I do it all? How is it possible to balance a full-time job, two children, two businesses, two trustee positions, my school governorship, not to mention my work within schools and other charity commitments, and one husband? I wish I had a one-size-fits-all type of answer, but unfortunately I don't. Everyone has different commitments and priorities, and I see balance as something that is very personal to each individual which can be made up of a multitude of different things.

The best advice I can offer if you have multiple responsibilities is to build your support network and continue to invest in it. The only reason I am able to manage so many different things is because of the support I have around me, and no, that doesn't mean I have an army of nannies and assistants. I'm talking about investing in a wider team of people who can help you, whether that's your partner, family, friends, babysitters, childminders, school mums, cleaners, coaches, mentors or anyone else you may need.

It is important to accept that at some point in your career there will be times when you alone cannot physically do everything you are either being asked to do or would like to do. In those situations you need to be honest with yourself about what you commit to or can realistically achieve. If you try to do it all, you will undoubtedly put yourself under a lot of stress and may even end up making yourself ill. I learned the word no far too late in my career and struggled as a result of that.

The remainder of my advice all centres around two themes that run concurrently throughout this book, and these are the value of planning and the value of building your various networks, albeit this time it's your support network as opposed to your business network – they are equally important.

From a planning perspective, start off by working out who you need to help you and when. The simplest method is to take your goals template discussed earlier and add a column for your support network, identifying whose help you'll need when, based on what you've got coming up. If you have blanks, then that's where you need to focus on building your network of support. You may also need to pay for the services of others to support you. Don't be daunted by the cost element; if you shop around or ask for recommendations from your network you will be surprised at your ability to keep costs down.

When it comes to children, you can look at sharing services with other parents to split costs. Explore all options and weigh up the pros and cons. You may need to be flexible and your choices may result in a few sacrifices in other areas of your life. Be prepared for that and accept that not everything is going to fall into place quite how you may like it to.

From a professional standpoint, if you are looking for a coach, try one who is newly qualified who needs to practise their skills. You can be savvy in terms of what you spend your money on here and investigate all options.

In terms of housework, consider what is good enough. Will 80% clean and tidy be OK or do you really need to bleach those skirting boards with a toothbrush every week (or is it just me that goes to that extreme!)? With other areas of support, do your homework and use your network to find recommended people who may be able to help you.

The biggest lesson I have learned is that no matter how much you think you might be able to, you cannot possibly do everything to the standard you would like to if you've got a lot going on. If you can learn to accept that this is OK, then you won't spend half your time feeling guilty or beating yourself up in your quest for domestic, work and family bliss. It is often only our own personal vision of who we're supposed to be that causes the horrible feelings of guilt, or worse still, failure. You are only human and you only have a set period of time to get things done. Complete what you can in the time you have to a standard that is acceptable to you, and yes I mean YOU, not others.

Below is the detail on how I try to balance it all in my life. I have tried and tested many different approaches through various periods of my career and life, and have rested on what works best for me and my family. Like all things, life is subject to change on a whim and no one has a crystal ball. Some of my examples or tips may apply to you now or in the future and some may not apply at all. However, I expect at some point in your life you will hit a busy period, therefore if anything I mention below helps to shape your thinking in some way, then this chapter was well worth writing!

Rules

In order to balance everything I have sets of rules for myself. Some I will not allow myself to compromise on, whereas others can be flexed. Any rule to do with the children's time cannot be compromised without their consent. When things have to give a little, I would rather the impact be on me than anyone else.

Over the past few years I have worked a four-day week at my day job. I won't compromise this for anyone. The fifth weekday is where I get to work on WeAreTheCity and the other responsibilities I have. It is also the day when I get to take the children to school and have their friends back after school. I have an open house policy on Fridays where as many of the children's friends can come back as they like. This is also my way of saying thank you to the other parents in the school who have supported me in my times of need.

I always make it to the children's events at school and I am very frank at my day job that I am not prepared to miss these events. Back in the early days of my career I used to disguise the children's events as doctor's appointments in my diary. At the time I thought that if I showed more commitment towards my children my employers would think that I wasn't dedicated enough to my career. Frankly, my rule should have been that I wouldn't work for a company that thought that way.

We always sit down together as a family unit on a Sunday for dinner, with no phones. I am a true believer that a family that eats together stays together. Sunday is our family time, and if I have things to do, I will get up earlier in the day to get them done or work later on Sunday evening. My mum often comes to help me if I have a lot going on; I couldn't survive without her support and help over the weekends.

Childcare

In terms of balancing childcare commitments with work, I chose to go with the services of a childminder who would work only for me in the early years of my children's lives. As my children required less one-on-one care, she would then be free to take on other children, which worked very well in terms of teaching my own children how to interact and share with others.

This is the woman I lured away from the nursery where she originally worked by offering to pay her the same salary for fewer days' work. I also offered to support her development while she worked for me and allowed her paid time off to progress her NVQ qualifications in other areas of childcare. As with all the people who have worked for me in the past, I treated her as a partner and not an employee. I allowed her to progress her career while giving her some of the balance she needed, and what I got in return was a happy childminder who has stayed with me and loved my children for over eleven years. Over that period her hours and responsibilities have changed, and I am lucky that she has been able to flex around our varying schedules and the changing needs of the children. She doesn't do any housework, but she will always offer to help me out with the odd post office run or pick-up if I'm stuck. She arrives at 6.30am to enable me to take the train to work by 7am which means I am at my desk in the City by 8am. She picks the children up from school, feeds them and leaves once Stewart and I are home. There were times, however, when she worked from 6am to 7.30pm in order for Stewart and me to fulfil our work commitments.

I realised a few years into my childcare arrangement that I hadn't built what I now know is an integral part of any support network, and this was a relationship with some of the other school mums. This was exceptionally difficult to do in the early years when I was never there, and even if I did manage to rearrange my diary in order to collect the children, I was always the one standing alone because I didn't know anyone. As I learned more about networking in my corporate career, I extended these skills and tried to build my network at the school. The concept was the same but the topics were different! Some of the mums turned out to be ex-City and had been in my shoes, facing similar challenges – that connection made it easier to build relationships. I had actually stayed away from anything remotely social because I'd been worried that the other mums might judge me because I had chosen my career above staying at home with my children. It was good to find out that this was definitely something in my head as opposed to reality.

The school mums are now an invaluable part of my support network and I wish I'd realised it sooner. As I got to know them better, I realised that this group of mothers were supporting each other, day in and day out, whether it was sharing challenges or tips or helping each other out. If you have children or are planning to, ensure you make the time to build relationships with other parents and create your school network early on. You will reap the benefits in terms of tips, support and the odd favour, and just be sure to return the favours when you can!

Spic and span - not necessarily

Before I had children, my house looked like a show home. I would spend hours puffing cushions, smoothing beds and polishing worktops. As soon as the children arrived, my house was trashed and probably will be in varying degrees until the moment they move out (if they move out!). What starts with an abundance of everything baby soon morphs into toys that take two months to put together and contain little bits that live and multiply in your carpet.

At first I maintained my efforts to keeping things clean and tidy thinking that I could have children *and* my show home. I learned quickly, and nowadays I am just happy to settle for clean. Tidy is not something I think I will ever see again until Stewart and I live in a two-bedroom bungalow on our own when we retire. I used to have a cleaner however, she left me – or should I say she left my children – therefore I now do it myself. I actually enjoy cleaning, which may seem surprising given my history of cleaning with my mum as a child. As a master multitasker, when I am cleaning I put in a bit more effort so it doubles up as a weekly workout too.

In terms of other household chores, I do have an ironing man. I am not sure if he actually does the ironing himself or whether he is just the delivery guy, but either way if I lost everything tomorrow, he would be one of the last people I would let go because I detest ironing!

Lots to do - write it down

My mum often reminds me that the first thing I ever wrote at age three was a to-do list. I think it's fair to say that being busy makes up the very essence of who I am. I still write lists to this day (and not just for me, but for my family and mentees!). I have copious numbers of little A5 black moleskin notebooks that contain lines and lines of things I need to do, and that way nothing slips through the gaps. Every morning on the way to work I check my list, adding and crossing things off. It gives me great pleasure to cross things off knowing they are done.

My biggest tip here is if you are managing multiple things, write them down and ensure you review your lists in the morning and evening. If you get so much as a five-minute gap, pull your list out and see if there is anything you could potentially get done. Keeping lists and using these as a tool to manage a wide variety of tasks can really help you to manage your multiple tasks and commitments.

Planning

At least once a month Stewart and I take an hour out to review our life plan. This incorporates everything from where we buy services from, to changing cars, houses, career moves, holidays and anything else that may affect our lives. If we are dealing with a larger project, eg. for WeAreTheCity, we have been known to take a day off in the week while the children are at school to hold our own strategy meeting (very romantic, I know!).

On a weekly basis, generally on Sunday afternoons after dinner, we sit down as a family and review our respective diaries for the next two weeks ahead. This includes the kids' diaries which on occasions are busier than ours! That way we ensure we have adequate cover in order for all of us to fulfil our individual commitments.

Prioritising

When prioritising, I tend to use the following guidelines when reviewing my workload (both life and work). Priority is given to the children, the job that pays the bills, and things that may affect my income and ultimately my health. I have learned that without a healthy me, nothing gets done, so that needs to stay high on the priority list. If I have made commitments to see people or attend an event, if I am feeling pressured I will question the value of doing that versus the time commitment. Do I really need to go, or is this something I can reschedule to a less busy period?

Busy periods

Busy times tend to come in waves and can be slightly unpredictable. You can plan for the things you know are coming (and if you have your goal plans mapped out as advised in the previous chapter, you will know roughly when these are). That's not to say that the odd unknown drama won't surface at some point and throw everything off track.

Managing a hefty to-do list and conflicting priorities takes dedication and focus. It is, of course, you yourself who sets your to-do list and you should be the one who sets your own priorities – bear this in mind when others are trying to inflict their not so well thought-through deadlines on to you. Question the urgency in requests from others. Even at work, I always question those who tell me things are urgent. Who said it's urgent and why? If it's the CEO that's one thing, but more often than not timing can be negotiated with those further down the line. Don't be afraid to push back and ask.

Avoiding burn out

There have been times in my career when I have almost worn myself into the ground by trying to juggle it all. After a few epic fails, I have learned to listen to my body and observe my behaviours to understand when I need to slow down. Listening to your body is as important as listening to the voice in your head that is telling you you are doing too much. Ignore these voices at your peril.

A few years back I was experiencing a period of extreme stress due to conflicting priorities, which was mostly my own fault as I hadn't quite learned to say no at that point. My brain had become clouded by the endless tasks I needed to complete to deliver everything to everyone. Even when I wrote it all down it seemed insurmountable. Earlier in my career I would have just thrown myself into these tasks, worked every hour I could muster and no doubt ended up sick as a dog as a consequence.

This time I did the opposite. I booked a cheap flight and went to Spain for 36 hours just to be out of my environment. This provided me with some much-needed thinking time and gave me a chance to prioritise what really needed doing and, most importantly, by when. I returned completely refreshed and rested, and probably got more done over the next two days than if I had stayed home stressing about how I was going to do it all. My big tip for you here is know when you need a break and take it! It doesn't even have to be overnight, but getting away from home to a different physical environment can be really helpful.

Guilt

This is a tough one. I have felt guilty since the moment I had my children, mostly because I wanted a career too and I knew that there would be times when both would need to be compromised. Feeling guilty is something that has never gone away for me. When I am at work, I think I should be with the children, and on occasions when I am with the children, I think I should be at work. There is no sweet-tasting pill that deals with this one, it is just something that you have to learn to deal with based on the choices you've made. The more comfortable you can be with the decisions you have made, the less guilt I expect you will feel. And remember that you don't need to defend your decisions to anyone, they are your decisions.

Taking time out

Taking time out for friends and family is hugely important for balance, so whatever you do, do not cancel those interactions from your life for sustained periods of time, even if you are ridiculously busy. You may need to think about alternative ways that you can be more savvy with your time. I arrange a quarterly dinner with my key networking contacts to ensure we remain connected and so they know that I am making time for them. Every six weeks I book in a family dinner, either away from home or family members take it in turns to host. I have also been known to tell friends and family that I may be going off the radar for a couple of months while I finish a particular project so they don't take my silence personally. Communication is key. If you tell friends and family that you are about to hit a busy period, they are more likely to understand and often they will offer to help you out too.

Asking for help

Another thing that many people are not very good at is asking for help from others. Just accept there will be times when you alone cannot conquer the world, and that extra pair of hands will make all the difference.

I have listened to so many people wax lyrical about all the things they have to do and you know they need help in some form, but they just won't ask. This seems to be a particular habit for those women who are juggling careers, caring responsibilities and other external responsibilities. I say, sod pride! If you need help, ask for it. Remember that if you don't ask, you won't get. Be sure to let your support network know that should they hit a busy period, you will be happy to chip in to help them too – and above all, ensure you honour that commitment.

Technology is a time saver

When I am on the train I am generally switching between two phones – one for work and one for personal things. The downside to this is that I don't have time to do other things like reading books or newspapers. I tend to rely on Twitter for headlines and breaking news.

I manage my three different email accounts via my smart phone. I tend to get about 100 emails a day for WeAreTheCity and at least 10 via LinkedIn. My day job can vary. When I am particularly busy I will put an out of office message on my personal email accounts stating that it may take me a day or so to get back to people.

I see free moments while commuting, eg. walking to work, as an opportunity to be communicating with people, either by phone or via email. How I haven't been run over in the City yet I don't know, because I am permanently head-down on my phone!

I often text rather than call my contacts. People tend to be more succinct over text than over the phone which makes it easier to get things done.

I order my shopping online, and tend to work in pockets in the evenings and weekends when the children are doing other activities. I rarely watch TV unless there is a documentary I particularly want to see. If the children are watching TV I tend to be on my laptop at the same time, answering emails, writing articles, reviewing board papers or updating my various social media channels.

I use technology where I can. Internet banking, train times, diet trackers – if it's on a phone app that makes my life easier, works on the go and saves time, then I'm using it!

Holidays

As a family, we rarely go on holiday for longer than four days. I like it because it gives the family lots of mini breaks, but more importantly for me personally it is the longest period of time I can go before my brain starts whirring with ideas again. Sometimes having such a strong network has a little bit of a downside, because whenever I do come up with an idea I am lucky enough to be able to mobilise these ideas very quickly through my contacts. It doesn't take long for an idea to become a reality, and before I know it, I have created something else I then need to maintain. So as backwards as it sounds, I need to keep the time away to a minimum to avoid accidently creating more work for myself once I get back!

I also ensure that I book shorter overnight breaks, eg. a night away at a hotel or a visit to friends or family. This takes the family away from our business at home and stops me from feeling like there are other things I should be doing. These are 'no technology' breaks – no laptops, Kindles or playing on phones, just family time.

Sleep

I have to have at least eight hours of sleep a night. If I don't, I am not as productive the next day. I try not to work right up to the point where I fall asleep otherwise my mind continues to work, albeit lying down with no laptop!

Generally, I get up around 5.45am each day, often seven days a week. Now that my daughters are slightly older they tend to get up before I go to work which means I get to see them. When they were younger and I was in my 'career is everything' mode, I would be gone before they were awake and came home when they were just going to bed. Those were hard times when I lived for the weekends to be able to spend quality time with them. I wish I could get that time back, children grow up so very fast.

At the weekend I get up at the same time. This gives me two to three hours to clear my personal emails before my children get up. Once they are up, we are on family time unless they choose to go to a club or do something that allows me to get on with other things.

I sleep with a notepad in my bedroom drawer. I do suffer with bouts of insomnia and often come up with my best ideas in the middle of the night. If I don't write them down they are gone by the morning. I have read back some pretty random things the next day, but I'm sure they were brilliant ideas at 2am that morning! Most recently, and thanks to a wonderful coach called Justine Lutterod of Synchronous Leadership, I have discovered a meditation and mindfulness tool called "Headspace". I am finding this tool (and phone app) a massive aid for times when I feel like I just cannot switch off.

If I have mission-critical things to do, I have on occasion stayed up late to complete them. If I try to sleep with urgent to-dos on my mind, I won't sleep well. If I have to stay up late I will review my diary in the morning to see if I can postpone any early morning meetings to later on in the day.

Spare time

As kids get older they go to bed later which means that I get more time with them during the week, but it also means that any time I used to have to myself on weekday evenings at home has almost disappeared. My evenings are generally dedicated to their various demands and needs.

When I do have any spare time, I like to run. I have always struggled with my weight, and I got into running after both of my pregnancies to get the baby weight off. I enjoy the freedom I feel while I'm running when I'm not at the mercy of timelines, to-do lists or instructions. I can just put my trainers on and run, and if I want to turn left or right I can, I am in total control. I rarely wear a watch when I'm running because it's the only time when I allow myself to lose the concept of time, if that makes any sense at all.

Every Sunday afternoon I take an hour out for myself for what I call maintenance (basically, pampering time!). This is my chance to prepare for the week ahead in terms of hair, the upcoming week's wardrobe and any other girly upkeep I want to do, and hopefully relax a little bit too! Despite the fact that I love being around other people, I also really enjoy my own company and a chance to do what I want to do, with no real outcomes needed.

Doing it all

When I'm at work, I am fully at work and totally in my corporate zone. I will only check Twitter or my personal emails during the morning and at lunchtime or if I am walking between buildings. I get in an hour earlier than I have to each morning because I enjoy the quiet time in the office. I sometimes use this time to arrange my week so I can be as effective as possible.

In order to continuously grow my network, I meet people before work, at lunchtime and sometimes on the way home. When I am particularly busy I will restrict these meetings to 30 minutes. I never go to lunch for longer than 45 minutes unless it's a first meeting. People tend to get to the point quicker and I find I actually get more done when I am working to a tighter meeting timeframe.

I always try to see people that contact me but there is never enough time in the day so I use Skype and other online tools to communicate with people or invite them to events where I am speaking.

So can you have it all?

From where I sit, the answer is yes and no. On occasions I experience the rare feeling that everything is in its box and organised for the following week. The house is tidy, the washing is done, the kids are clean and I have a scrollable email inbox and checked-off to-do list. At work I am on top of my projects, WeAreTheCity is going well, and above all I am healthy and happy. This is the closest I get to my interpretation of having it all. I have learned to enjoy those moments as they are pretty rare, but I have also learned not to beat myself up should something fall out of that box.

So many women put pressure on themselves to be everything to everyone. These are often our own measures of what success looks like for a working parent or busy woman and not what anyone else would have expected from us given the amount we are no doubt juggling. I cannot tell you how many cans of dry shampoo I have used since its creation, or how many times I have gone out of the door with the wrong suit jacket or discovered the odd ladder in my tights. In the early years, it was more likely to be baby milk on my suit or Weetabix in my hair. You have to learn to accept that if you are juggling multiple things, there are occasions when something has to give and you won't be perfect all of the time.

Balance will always be a difficult one to achieve or advise on. It's easier if you try to recognise when you are likely to experience periods when your own perception of healthy balance will be compromised and plan for that period accordingly.

The key message is don't put unnecessary pressure on yourself to be perceived as a superwoman. There will be times when you can't do it all and times when you can. Don't forget to celebrate the moments when you feel you are the closest to achieving balance as you are ever going to get, and recognise what it took to get to that point. Pat yourself on the back, and take comfort in the knowledge that there are millions of women all over the world facing the same sorts of challenges. Leverage as many ideas and tips from others as you can, and don't give yourself such a hard time. You are only human.

IT'S YOUR TURN TO SHINE

"Your boat doesn't come in, you have to swim out to it" – Nettie Rosen

(my nan's own version of a Jonathan Winters quote)

If I managed to survive the corporate jungle despite all my ups and downs, so can you. However, survival and thriving comes with a few firm commitments on your part.

First, you need to commit to grabbing your career by the horns. It's not just about reading this book and putting it on a shelf thinking that some career fairy is going to build your action plan for you or that your boss is going to sort you out. This is your career and it certainly doesn't belong to anyone else, and I am sorry to burst any perceived bubble, but that career fairy is in fact YOU. The day you start your plan is today, not tomorrow. Whether it's as simple as joining WeAreTheCity or investigating a network or updating your LinkedIn profile, a start is a start. That said, if you are really serious about your career and achieving success, don't delay the bigger planning exercise. Structure equals success, and I know you want to succeed in your career otherwise you wouldn't have bought this book and read it all the way to the end!

You also know that you are going to have to muster commitment, passion and strength because the road towards success is not always an easy one. I will tell you the same thing that my mum told me all those years ago when I was a little girl: if you really want something in life, work hard. Put the effort in and you can and will achieve what you want.

Visualise it, plan for it and take every opportunity that comes your way, even if it doesn't quite seem to fit in with your existing plans. I have often ventured down unknown paths purely for the experience, and now when I look back I realise that those paths led me to new lessons, new people and new opportunities.

The choices you make and paths you take will involve an element of risk. Nothing is achieved without risk! Calculate it and make your decision. Who wants to look back 30 years down the line saying "I wish I had..."? If it feels right, then do it. If your gut is telling you otherwise, listen to it. Your gut instinct is your best friend. I ignored that piece of advice several times in my career and still regret it.

If others doubt you or try to derail you in some way, take it in your stride. Play smart and don't react! Use their doubt to fuel your ambition to prove them wrong. You are the true judge of your own abilities and sometimes you need to treat the opinions of others as just noise. Thank them for their input and move on with your plans. Know where you want to go and stay focused. Always remember that you are the maker of your own music. If things don't work out the first time, then dust yourself off and learn from it.

Mistakes are often the best way of learning and they are not to be feared. No one is perfect or able to be everything to everyone or to balance it all. Be fair to yourself – if you look inside yourself and know that you are putting the maximum effort into all you do, or that you know you made the right decision, then you are on the right track. Every step, no matter how small, is progress.

In relation to others you meet, see every person as a golden opportunity. Learn about people. Listen, connect and open every conversation with what you can give to that individual. Connect people and raise the profile of others. The good deeds you do will come back to benefit you over time.

Success in your career is not just about having a structured plan, it is about building a strong network of others that can and will help you. From your perspective, it is about being focused, working hard and seizing opportunities. Approach everything you do with a positive outlook, give every task 120%, be open to change and when the waves come, just ride them – no sea remains choppy forever.

There will no doubt be times when you feel like the world is against you and you are not making progress, but it will pass. The one thing you mustn't do is quit. If you have goals and dreams then no matter what gets in the way, you must return to them and never give up trying.

Now you have the inside track on a few of the situations that may arise in your corporate career, and if they do, you know where to go for help. From networks to mentors to websites, there is no excuse for sitting back and not leveraging the support around you. You also know where to go to grow your career and you have a few methods and ideas to get you started.

If you need a little more help and structure, you can join my Pipeline Academy or attend one of my inspiration days. More information is available on www.thepipelineacademy.com.

Regardless of what you intend to do next, I sincerely hope that you drew inspiration from this book and that you go on to achieve your own personal definition of success, whatever that may be.

Best of luck and keep pushing your boundaries.

Vanessa

SO WHAT HAPPENED NEXT?

Writing a book, especially when it is autobiography, is an extremely cathartic experience. I feel like I have almost lived the past 25 years twice! From tears of sorrow to laughter, I have felt so many different emotions over the past six months as this book has sprung to life. Seeing some of my life and career experiences on paper has also made me realise just how much I have managed to pack in in such a relatively short period of time. I honestly haven't stopped!

It was this realisation that led me to conclude that I actually need a break. My reward for completing the book and working so hard is going to be an opportunity to hang up my own 'heels of steel' and put my flats on for a while.

So, after leaving my last corporate assignment and finally learning to say no to a number of other opportunities, I am now set to start my six month sabbatical. Even I can't believe it – a whole six months off! We can forget the no pay aspect as that's the less glamorous part of the plan.

So over the next six months, I plan to use this precious time to travel with my children and take them on that three week trip around Europe we have always spoken about. When I return in September, I will be investing more of my time in WeAreTheCity and Careers City as both seem to be at their tipping point in terms of success (4 million hits per month and rising!). In fact, my plans to double the traffic and members was achieved one year ahead of target. Aside from growing both businesses, I plan to travel and promote "Heels of Steel" in as many countries and organisations that will have me. Above all, during these six months, I plan to be able to spend time doing what I love the most, which is giving back to my charities and supporting others (especially the youngsters) with their career aspirations.

As for what comes next after the next six months, for now, who knows? Perhaps Dorothy has finally reached her own Emerald City and will choose to stay there full time.

Until we find out or the next chapter unfolds, here's to the future, the success of yours and the sanctum of mine.

Warmest,

Vanessa

RESOURCES

Careers and Networking Advice

For networking groups, advice, jobs, events and career support for women – www.wearethecity.com

For mentoring, webinars and coaching – www.thepipelineacademy.com

For networking advice, visit www.smarter-networking.co.uk or www.lopata.co.uk/

Leadership Advice

Institute of Leadership & Management – www.i-l-m.com

The Centre for Creative Leadership – www.ccl.org

For general advice in relation to work – www.acas.org.uk

For support on mission statements and goals – www.stephencovey.com

Building Profile

Domain registrations – www.123-reg.co.uk

Website design – www.fiddydesign.com

Creating your blog – www.wordpress.com

Headshots – www.johncassidyheadshots.com

Tailoring – www.nooshin.co.uk

Business cards – www.moo.com

Writing a book – www.bookmidwife.com

Giving Back

To learn more about charities/community service – www.wearethecity.com/giving-back

Mentoring – www.getmentoring.org or www.mentoring.org or www.cherieblairfoundation.org

For trustee positions in the UK – www.trusteenet.org.uk/

For school governor positions in the UK – www.nga.org.uk/

For board advice and positions – www.nonexechub.com

To donate money – www.thebiggive.org.uk

ABOUT THE PIPELINE ACADEMY

What is the Pipeline Academy?

The Pipeline Academy is a coaching, mentoring and connections club for aspiring leaders that provides career advice, tools and learning opportunities for its members. The Pipeline Academy is led by Vanessa Vallely and is only open to a limited number of individuals. The aim of the academy is to help to build the next generation of corporate leaders by supplementing their careers with a myriad of tips and advice from individuals with solid track records of success within their corporate fields. Entrance to the Pipeline Academy is by application only.

Who should apply?

The Pipeline Academy is looking for talented individuals who are serious about taking their careers to the next level and ultimately aiming for leadership roles. Our ideal candidates are people who want some learning through a structured approach but who are also enthusiastic about building their networks and learning through the experiences of others.

Individuals at all levels are encouraged to apply.

How long is the programme?

There is a six-month minimum commitment to membership in the Pipeline Academy. After that it's up to you how long you stay!

What is the time commitment?

The Pipeline Academy initially meets in person in central London for a half-day workshop over a weekend. Following the workshop, the Pipeline Academy will require approximately three hours per month which includes webinars and the monthly coaching session. Additional time participating in networking events is at the discretion of the member.

How do I apply or find out more information?

Please visit www.thepipelineacademy.com for an application form or more information about The Pipeline Academy.

ABOUT VANESSA VALLELY
(THE FINAL BIO - OR IS IT?)

Vanessa Vallely is a recognised expert in person-to-person business networking, online branding and a sought-after motivational speaker. She is regarded as one of the most well-networked women in and out of the City and is passionate about sharing her know-how and experiences with others.

In 2008, Vanessa started the networking site: www.wearethecity.com as a vehicle to help other City women connect and grow professionally and personally. WeAreTheCity (WATC) receives more than 4 million hits per month and has an average of 65,000 unique visitors.

Today, WATC has become the 'little black book' for London's female workforce. More than 10,000 members rely on WATC for information ranging from professional to personal, to connect with others or to access interests that are core to working in the City. Vanessa also recently created www.careerscity.co.uk which is a job board aimed at raising the visibility of the opportunities open to women at all stages of their careers.

Vanessa has worked tirelessly to further the diversity agenda across the City and beyond. To that end, Women in Banking and

Finance (WiBF) recognised her achievements with the 2011 Women's Champion Award. In 2009, Vanessa co-founded the City-wide diversity forum The Networks of Networks (TNON). The TNON includes diversity heads and heads of women's networks from 40 FTSE firms.

As a testimony to her achievements, Vanessa has appeared on many lists of top business people in the City, including: Financial News Top 100 Rising Star across Europe, Africa and EMEA; Financial News Top 100 Women in Finance; The International Alliance for Women's Top 100 Women; The Womensphere Award for Leadership and most recently Brummels Top 30 Inspirational Women in the City.

Companies, charities and various media channels have invited Vanessa to speak about The Power of Networking and The Power of Profile as well as about her 25 years of experience in the City and financial services.

Vanessa is committed to community service and is a non-executive director for Prostate Cancer UK, the organisation behind the Movember movement, and National Youth Musical Theatre (NYMT). She is also the Pearly Queen of the City of London which represents a fundamental aspect of London's community service heritage.

Vanessa has recently written her first book *Heels of Steel* and launched The Pipeline Academy which aims to help the next generations of talent achieve their career goals and become the leaders of the future.

www.WeAreTheCity.com